Objects & Us

Gus
Casely-
Hayford

Thames
&Hudson

V&A

Objects & Us

Why Things Matter

Contents

Preface

Like many great fashion designers, Cristóbal Balenciaga did not hail from a fashion dynasty. He was born in 1895 in Getaria, a small fishing village on Spain's Urola coast. And from relatively humble beginnings, he succeeded in securing for himself a position within one of the most elitist and insular areas of the arts. He crafted breathtaking dresses and dazzling collections, building an unrivalled reputation and eventually ending his career as one of the most respected fashion designers of a truly stellar generation that included Chanel, Givenchy and Dior. Balenciaga's creative drive was not born of a hunger for fame, money or influence; rather, it was born of love. His mother was a seamstress who occasionally made dresses for the women of Getaria. She taught her son to sew and would allow the young Cristóbal to observe the sartorial transformation of the fishermen's wives as their dresses were conceived, crafted and fitted. It would instil in him a love of making, and of its power – if only momentarily – to change lives.

Balenciaga created clothes as a way of being and as a way of reconnecting with his beginnings. He designed exquisite dresses as gifts to his clients, as tools of transformation. His designs seemed to bubble and effervesce from somewhere deep within, eventually erupting out of him. At his best, he would imagine and then organically engineer dresses like a sculptor, arranging discrete slices of fabric, one upon another, often without pre-planning. It was a technique that allowed him to create garments that were simply unlike those of other designers. His cutting, his silhouettes and his shapes would be copied and envied by his peers. To his friends and colleagues within the fashion industry, he became known as 'the master of us all'. And yet, Cristóbal Balenciaga sought little or no publicity, was deeply introverted, and rarely spoke publicly – and in his final years, he expressed a desire for his label to die with him. He would leave behind some of the most innovative, important and considered garments of the twentieth century.

This cerise silk taffeta dress is one of the many sartorial triumphs of Balenciaga's career: it is an engineering miracle. Acquired by a British debutante in 1954, it could only have been conceived and chosen to stun. Its shape, its flounces, its vivid colour were inspired by the gowns of the belle epoque, but its most brilliant innovation is hidden to all but the wearer. It did not rely on restrictive corsetry but discreetly held its shape in ways that were radically freeing for the wearer. Brilliant cutting and subtle internal ribs replaced the conventional internal scaffolding of Victorian womenswear, to retain the shape and gain freedom of movement. Balenciaga had found a way to balance respect for heritage with innovation. In its being, the dress spoke to the needs of bodies and to the possibilities of fantastic design.

And that this exquisitely engineered object would become one of the points of inspiration for the striking silhouette and textured exteriors of the V&A East Museum somehow feels very right. Reminiscent of a garment, the

CRISTÓBAL BALENCIAGA (1895–1972)
Evening dress, 1954. Silk taffeta

folded external façade forms a protective outer layer for the building and its contents. The sculptural form gives a sense of the interior volume and the unfurling spaces in between the façade and its steel skeleton. Internally, an open sequence of galleries is arranged around a central core, accessed by exposed stairways to encourage a free flow of movement and chance encounters with both objects and people.

Creativity, that drive to make, can be powerful. It can present as desire, as a pathology, an ache, and as existential need; and our desire to possess or be close to beautifully conceived and crafted things, to collect them, to give them, to share them, is the matching need, deep and fundamental. It is simply something we must do.

Introduction

Human beings need a complex assortment of things to live well and lead fulfilling lives, and one of those things is undoubtedly culture. Yet, we rarely speak about art and design, about culture, in terms of need. Although most of us would accept the importance of creativity in our lives, we often think of art and beautiful things as a luxury, as perhaps even a little frivolous. But the creation and appreciation of man-made objects is common to every society. It is one of a small number of behaviours we share with our earliest human ancestors, with people from all walks of life and class spanning millennia. If we were to try to define humanity, we might say that, while we demonstrate a consistent drive to be destructive, we are also deeply creative and inventive. Before we can walk, before we can talk, we exhibit the compulsion to create, to make, to craft. It is one of the behavioural traits that define us as a discrete genus. Collecting, collating and arranging are equally old impulses, ancient fundamental human drives. Our pre-human ancestors left behind material patterns of collecting, seeming to attach value to things for their own sake. Every culture across history has collected; every society has imbued particular objects with special value and built systems and narratives to support their appreciation.

In 1943, two years after the United States entered the Second World War, and as the momentum began to swing behind the Allies, a brilliant American psychologist, Abraham Maslow, published his first essay on human need. It was perfectly timed. As many were beginning to dare to think about life beyond war, Maslow asked: what do humans *really* need? And how might we build a hierarchy of the things that are necessary for good, fulfilling lives to be led? Following the hardships and sacrifices of war, a discussion of humanity shaped through the lens of need felt like an important and worthwhile activity. Maslow's subsequent 'hierarchy of needs' crafted a framework of the things that humans require to be human: from the most basic, life-essential necessities that are critical to survival, to the elements that help to safeguard our security, to the things that make up the social fabric that underpins relationships, to the things that offer us self-actualization. Although this hierarchy was formulated as a pyramid, with the life-critical things at the base and the least immediately practical at the apex, Maslow came to believe that human beings might well sometimes choose beauty over warmth, religious expression over food and creative opportunity over comfort, because love, passion and culture are all critical for a good life.

In this book I have recast Maslow's hierarchy, identifying twelve human needs and pairing them with objects from the last 600 years of human history – the majority of them in the collection of the Victoria and Albert Museum (V&A) – to help us consider why these things and the human drive for creativity are important. My aim is to show how the products of art and design are not simply material evidence of the human story – that they are in fact necessary for us to *be* human. *Objects & Us* explores what makes certain objects important; from the humble to the magnificent, these are objects that can orientate and make sense of us. Culture is the exquisite shadow we cast upon the world, the mark humanity inevitably leaves behind, a magnificent manifestation of our existential needs. And perhaps the lens through which we can most tangibly understand our worth.

We need things. We need them for substantial, quantifiable reasons, but also for some deeply ineffable reasons too. And it is perhaps in moments of existential crisis when those reasons feel most tangible, when we are forced to consider what art might really mean to us; how for nations, communities and individuals, the great collections of art and material culture can offer a rare kind of connective tissue that can help us make sense of who we are. It can be symbolic, the knot that binds us, not just to each other, but also a mechanism for mapping our histories and changing selves.

On 30 September 1938, the distinctive silhouette of a Lockheed 14 emerged from between the clouds over West London and began its descent towards Heston Aerodrome. From the air, London, the most dynamic city on Earth, looked almost vulnerable. You could see its old bones mapped out around the lazy, looping bends of its river – its medieval villages, its Roman roads, its densely populated Victorian and Edwardian suburbs, the domes and towers of power, its vast commercial heart melting into the eastern smog of factories and big industry. And on that particular autumn afternoon, a palpable pall hung over the city: the anxiety of a populace awaiting bad news. As the plane taxied across the runway, the waiting crowd edged forward, leaving just enough space for the Lockheed's fourteen passengers to disembark. This was the third flight that the British prime minister, Neville Chamberlain, had taken to Europe in recent weeks on a humiliating odyssey in search of peace. He had in turn courted Benito Mussolini, Adolf Hitler and Édouard Daladier, the prime minister of France, but today the mood on board was different. Chamberlain was returning home with a signed agreement that he believed would avert another war – and would finally silence his many detractors.

Later that day, a visibly emotional and exhausted Prime Minister spoke from the steps of 10 Downing Street: 'My good friends, for the second time in our history, a British Prime Minister has returned from Germany bringing peace with honour. I believe it is peace for our time. We thank you from the bottom of our hearts. Go home and get a nice quiet sleep.' But not everyone was convinced of the tenability of Chamberlain's 'peace for our time'. Within hours, thousands had mobilized on Trafalgar Square, protesting loudly against the government's naivety, their chants wafting out across Whitehall and down the Mall. It was one of those moments when the gears of history seemed to shift palpably, when the moral authority of the government seemed to evaporate into the late afternoon air. And just yards from where the protestors gathered, the director of the National Gallery, Kenneth Clark, had consulted with his trustees and sanctioned the move of one of the world's great collections of paintings from central London in anticipation of war. Fifty paintings were moved that day as part of a set of plans that had been in development by Britain's national museum directors for years. Like many whose lives had spanned the darkest days of the First World War, they were already resigned to the inevitability of another global conflict. And perhaps naturally, the museum sector's first loyalty was to its collections – even at the cost of the government's embarrassment.

Perhaps for political reasons, the fifty paintings were returned to London later that very day, but a point had been made. This body of art underwrote Britain. It told and symbolized a national story in ways that felt only heightened by the threat of war. And so, a year later, as war was declared, slate mines in Wales – hundreds of miles from London – were filled with some of Britain's greatest treasures, and the National Gallery was emptied, shuttered and closed. Across central London, each of the other national museums implemented similar plans. The V&A, like the British Museum, filled underground passages and mothballed Tube stations across London, select country houses and those slate mines in Wales. The loss of this spiritual lodestone would not just be devastating for art history; it also had the potential to have a negative impact on the nation as a whole, in a time of need.

But people also missed art, and even in the opening years of the war, commentators reflected on the loss of loved cultural events from London life. It was not a campaign as such, more of a growing, ambient yearning that manifested itself in letters to the press and to arts venues: letters bemoaning the absence of beauty from people's lives; letters extolling the value of the arts, not just as entertainment or as a source of compelling narrative, but as a reservoir of the human spirit. It was a sentiment that grew into a wider discussion about the extrinsic merits of the arts as a potent morale galvanizer and social coagulant.

At the outbreak of war, the V&A had adopted a slightly different approach from the National Gallery. Sir Eric Maclagan, the V&A's director, was an interesting figure. During the First World War, he had held a senior role in the Ministry of Information, the government department tasked with communications and propaganda. Maclagan understood how narrative and culture might be deployed in aiding a war effort, and how effective culture could be in raising morale. Like Clark, he had withdrawn a substantial proportion of the V&A's most valuable and portable collection at the outbreak of hostilities (fig. 1), but critical sections of the V&A's library and many of its galleries remained in place, accessible to the public, even when Exhibition Road and Fulham Road

1.
Objects at the Victoria and Albert Museum are prepared for their removal and protection during the Second World War, London, England, *c.* 1939–45

sustained bomb damage. Alongside the galleries that were being used to shelter child refugees, its other ground-floor spaces were open. The V&A's trustees and director felt that the museum's collections could have a role to play in this chapter of Britain's history; and with many other venues closed, it made a powerfully defiant statement.

After joining the museum in 1905, Maclagan had slowly worked his way up through the ranks of the Department of Architecture and Sculpture. The year after he joined the museum, his department had begun the process of acquiring pieces of a medieval ceiling saved from the recently demolished Palacio de Altamira (Altamira Palace) in Torrijos, near Toledo in Spain (see page 155). Before its demolition, the palace had boasted four impressive towers, their interiors finished with ornate carved and painted ceilings. During the initial years of his employment, the V&A had embarked on a complex and painstaking programme of acquisition and detective work, slowly gathering sections of one of the exquisitely intricate ceilings and piecing it back together. Originally commissioned in the fifteenth century by Gutierre de Cárdenas, an ally of King Ferdinand II and Queen Isabella I, the ceiling was crafted from panels of painted and gilded Iberian pine and combines both Islamic and Christian decorative styles in a textile-like geometric arrangement. It would take years to reconstruct but was eventually completed and installed more than ten metres above one of the V&A's grandest galleries. And this beautiful, rare, fragile object was one of the many exhibits that would remain *in situ* for the duration of the Second World War. Maclagan, who had crafted communications strategies during the First World War, would have understood both the risks and the full significance of the ceiling staying in place.

Over the many months of the Blitz, the Luftwaffe dropped more than 20,000 bombs on London, killing more than 40,000 people and leaving behind thousands of devastated homes, businesses and families. Every organ of state, every vestige of governmental resource, every civic and municipal body was marshalled to the defence of the nation and its allies. The concentrated energies of the nation's leadership, the press, the financial bodies, manufacturing, industry, the Church were pressed into support of the war effort in what became the most complete and globalized war ever waged. And, when everything important felt at stake, the need for art in people's lives felt ever heightened. As the news of the horrendous daily losses from the front began to mount, as the cumulative impact of everyday hardships and sacrifices took an increasing toll, there grew a palpable anxiety: a blanket of communal emotional exhaustion began to pervade many communities. The British government knew that this was a war that would need to be waged and won, at least in part, in people's hearts and minds – and they looked at ways of lifting morale.

What were the touchstones that people might reach out to in this time of need? What were the narratives around which they might coalesce? It was here that art and culture suddenly felt more than important; they began to feel vital. There grew a broadly supported opinion that, despite the risks, more art should be shown in London's galleries – that the strategies deployed by the V&A at the outset of the war felt measured, appropriate and correct. So the National Gallery policy was reversed and selected works were returned from Wales – and for much of the remaining years of the war, thousands would queue everyday down the steps and across Trafalgar Square to see handfuls of paintings on the gallery's walls. As London dealt with the daily threat of the Blitz, its citizens yearned for these magnificent creative celebrations of humanity – and to leave our greatest treasures hidden deep in slate mines felt ultimately unsatisfactory.

Every museum seeks to balance the responsibility to protect and conserve its collections with the drive to share and make those same collections accessible. Many of the most august and respected institutions are united in their radical founding and enduring core public purpose of sharing. From the British Museum to the Smithsonian to the V&A, we are linked by continuing to value that aspiration for meaningful public engagement. And long histories of building relationships between collections and audiences have created a legacy: layers of accreted public affection, years of love imbibed by objects has changed the way we see them – and when, as in the Blitz, we needed to draw on that bank of fondness, our collections responded.

We have evolved a beautiful interdependence with objects – beyond the purely functional, beyond the purely aesthetic. Great art is rarely simply beautiful; amazing design is rarely just utilitarian: material culture is a crucible of shared stories, shared aspirations, triumphs and fears. It can act as a communal mirror, capturing and sharing how we feel about the world. We can choose to lock things away, to keep them safe, but that may serve gradually to decouple them from a human narrative. Art and material culture thrive on human attention – and we in turn thrive when exposed to great art.

Do we protect and conserve great works at all cost? Do we strive to limit their exposure to any kind of risk? Or do we best honour them by dramatically broadening access – by making them, whenever viable, available to our audiences? At V&A East – the V&A's newest outpost, made up of V&A East Museum and V&A East Storehouse – we looked at this seemingly binary set of choices and, after careful consideration, followed Maclagan's lead and decided on a third option. V&A East has chosen to invest in the collection through measured, thoughtful stewardship and radical, uncompromising but considered access. We have, like Maclagan, chosen both love of audience and love of collection, both public need and the needs of the rare, precious, world-class objects in our care. And it feels entirely appropriate that V&A East Storehouse is the new home of Gutierre de Cárdenas's great ceiling, where, restored, it looks vital and magnificent. I hope Maclagan would be delighted.

V&A East is a twenty-first-century celebration of the love that humans can hold for things – a platform for enjoying what close proximity to glorious objects can offer us; a new space dedicated to preserving and celebrating one of the world's great collections of art and design. V&A East Storehouse is an exquisite, open, shared public jewel box designed by Diller Scofidio + Renfro that places audiences at the heart of the collection, where they can enjoy unprecedented public access to the objects held within and witness how they are cared for (fig. 2).

This experiential storehouse is paired with an experimental, partnership-based museum and exhibition platform designed by O'Donnell + Tuomey. Through our programming, we hope to forge communal engagement with our immensely varied collection of objects while acknowledging their often complex and difficult histories, making space for new relationships of equity, empathy and openness between different cultures, communities, artists and makers from around the world. One of the most rewarding aspects of my job has been taking objects from our

2.

Example of the mini curated displays 'hacked' into the sides and ends of storage racking in the central Weston Collections Hall at V&A East Storehouse, 2025 collections into East London schools, visiting a hundred schools in the four boroughs that surround our sites. These encounters exposed tens of thousands of young people to our collections, from deliciously, richly decorated Indian jewellery (fig. 3) to a nineteenth-century African box created to hold gold dust (fig. 28). They also exposed me to the power of the stories behind these objects to engage and inspire.

In this book, I reconsider Maslow's hierarchy of need through the lens of culture to show the necessary role that art and creativity have played in our human story. And by deploying Maslow's hierarchy as a framework for thinking about culture and our creative drive, it offers us an elegant way to understand the world and our place within it – a way to get close to what is important to us and, crucially, to get close to some truly wonderful things and consider why they really matter.

Within his hierarchy of human need, Maslow's core theme was that community is fundamental to humanity. The opening chapter of this book, on warmth, examines how migrant communities have helped everyone understand the importance of hospitality and welcome. Consecutive chapters examine health and the impact of art and design on well-being in society, before moving into the necessary but mysterious – even fearful – realm of sleep and the creative possibilities of escape. We then focus on how politics has played a strong and complex part in helping to shape notions of creativity, habitat and property. The narrative then subtly shifts to our interior drives, by looking at confidence, followed by breath and respect. The final chapters consider some of the drivers of social creativity, such as family, food and a sense of purpose.

We come into the world alone, and, from birth, we instinctively try to bridge the gap between us and others. We naturally seek to connect with our parents, our families, our neighbours, our communities. But even when we are most successful in this endeavour, how do we measure and corroborate the quality of the connections we make? Do we ever really know what others are thinking or feeling? We can spend time with others, but how often do we share our most profound understandings, feelings or perspectives on the world? In order to share how we feel, the nature of our emotions, our fears and desires, we need to build common reference points, emotional way-markers. Perhaps that is one of the many wonderful things that great culture can deliver: a space in which to understand and empathize, a means to capture and share feelings, a mechanism for understanding each other and ourselves, for navigating our past and positing our futures. The things we make are the media of possibility, of understanding, of dreams, desires, fears and remembrance. A strange synaptic evolutionary anomaly that has helped us gain a profound abstract understanding of who we are; and, in what follows here, I will explore some glorious examples of when we have done that best. I hope to show not only how important art, creativity and thereby 'things' are to us, but also why we just need them.

So, these are a handful of V&A East stories of art. Stories of why we have made art and stories of how art made us. A history of how we have invested in creating, collecting and protecting art – and of how these objects have repaid and reciprocated our love by being a loyal, constant witness, our guide and inspiration. This is a story of why we need art, and why art needs us. It is a love letter to all those truly exceptional things that seem to accrete and hold onto histories, and which, when we ask, yield their stories in beguiling and beautiful ways.

3.

LEFT AND RIGHT: Earrings, *c.* 1880. Gold with granulations, 1.5 cm (diameter). CENTRE: Ear ornament, *c.* 1885. Gold or silver-gilt with wire, 1.9 cm (diameter)

Warmth

Clothing has often been a means of establishing continuity in a new setting, with immigrant communities bringing with them textiles and textile traditions that endure across generations and straddle thousands of miles. Starting with the Huguenot community in London in the eighteenth century and the dazzling innovations of Spitalfields silk, this is the story of how communities fleeing hostility and seeking opportunity have settled abroad and brought their expertise to bear on the making-cultures of their new homes. Focusing on the vital warmth of community, it touches on Althea McNish's role in helping the textile culture of Britain shake off its post-Second World War sobriety, and how designers respond to similar impulses today.

The British are an island people. The British story is one of trade and migration, of the constant ebb and flow of peoples, goods and ideas. Modern Britain came into being through exchange, through the co-development of new ways of thinking. Many of the most significant cultural narratives of our national story began beyond our shores. The British are Normans from France, they are Saxons and Angles from Northern Europe, they are Roman, they are Yoruba, they are Sinhalese, they are Han: we are British. The British are a glorious, cultural mix of peoples of diverse origins and varied ways of living, who have made their homes, offered their labour and shared their talents to make Britain. Like other European nations, Britain adopted a national flag in the early nineteenth century: the Union Jack, which merged several – although, significantly, not all – regional flags. Not just a representation of overarching characteristics (like the tricolours of our neighbours), but a multicultural pennant – layers of discrete identities thrust into a dynamic relationship, one upon another, until they each yielded enough to form a single flag. The Union Jack signifies complexity and diversity, tolerance and tension; it is a flag that speaks to the dissonances and the demographic churn that have consistently underwritten national narratives. This localized imperialism speaks to the defining political philosophy that would characterize a nation and its expanding global influence and power: a cosmopolitan cultural confidence that has fuelled pride, ambition and national hubris.

On Empire Day at the height of Britain's imperial influence, almost a third of the world's children would stand to sing 'God Save the Queen'.[1] For much of the nineteenth century, Britain was unchallenged militarily, unrivalled at sea; Britain's laws, language and cultural mores had spread around the globe. In turn, there was the corollary of that outward influence: Britain's domestic culture had become one of the most dynamic, diverse, cosmopolitan and creative environments on the planet. The V&A's collections tell that story of exchange, of empire, of enslavement, of trade, of migration and refuge; stories of making that are realized in gold and mahogany, in ivory and silks – a vast, complex material culture that tells both British and global stories.

And it was in Britain's port cities that those creative narratives came into being in their most dynamic form. Liverpool, Bristol, Hull and, of course, London – our capital city with its vast East End planted beyond the city walls, an enduring melting pot for migrants and transient communities. East London was not just the place where the global goods were docked, processed and sold; it also housed communities of recent migrants and refugees, eventually coming to accept each discrete group of new arrivals as its own. And so, today, East London has no need to excavate layers of material archaeology in search of these histories because you can observe the residual cultural hybridities alive in its communities. A living history of Saxon settlements, of Huguenot refugees, the pockets of Ashkenazi Jews, the communities of Chinese, Irish, Bengalis, West Africans, Eastern Europeans and so many more.

Warmth is a critical component of the East London story – a cultural history shaped by migrants and newcomers. Its peoples not only sought the warmth and sanctuary of the area's cultural diversity, they were also in part defined by the varied fabrics that they introduced and traded, by the textiles and garments they would conceive and design to protect us from the inclement easterly winds. Even today, East London's markets remain a tangible commercial and creative celebration of the city's sartorial complexity.

When, in 1685, King Louis XIV of France revoked the centuries-old protections afforded to Calvinist Protestants, or Huguenots, it led to a period of profound instability across Europe. Along with the destruction of their churches and confiscation of their properties, the Huguenots suffered systematic campaigns of sustained persecution. Hundreds of thousands fled France, seeking asylum in cities across Northern Europe, some carrying great wealth, knowledge and a rich portfolio of skills. This period of migration and economic instability would also foster unprecedented opportunity and invention as new creative perspectives and intellectual innovations that were forged among the social tumult catalysed economies – this was the very birth of the Enlightenment. Of the thousands who sought refuge in Britain, perhaps the most influential were the Huguenot silk-weavers, who would make Spitalfields, East London, their home.

Britain had long sought to build and strengthen its silk production. Silk was one of the most prized commodities of the age. A century before the arrival of the Huguenots, James I had famously planted 100,000 mulberry trees adjacent to Hampton Court Palace in an extravagant attempt to strengthen British silk production by growing acres of the silkworms' only food source. However, like so many similar British ventures of the period, it floundered.[2] But silk *was* worth the investment. A light, elegant fabric, its tightly packed fibres are naturally breathable and temperature-regulating, with the ability to trap a layer of insulating air close to the skin. While it could help to cool the body, it could also provide warmth – an especially important quality for the newly arrived residents of East London. And when combined in layers with wool or cotton, it could deliver very effective insulation indeed.

The Huguenots included among their numbers some of the most successful cloth merchants, master weavers and designers in Europe; and by the mid-eighteenth century, London was home to craftsmen and women of Huguenot descent who were leading exponents of the latest continental style. Within a generation, they had changed the scale and productivity of the East London textile trade. Their arrival anticipated that of a complete silk-making sector. Among the immigrant families were 'throwsters', skilled in crafting and twisting silk

4.

JAMES LEMAN (1688–1745)

LEFT: Design commissioned by Isaac Tuille, a leading Convent Garden mercer, London, 15 July 1709. Watercolour and bodycolour on paper. RIGHT: Length of dress fabric, 1709. Lampas weave silk with brocading

filaments into threads, and vast numbers of journeymen weavers, who toiled for long hours, crafting lengths of cloth for scant reward. There were celebrated makers such as Edward Peck, whose innovative techniques for colouring silk resulted in fought-over crimson cloths that would make his fortune. Then there were the pattern drawers like James Leman, who produced complex works for elite markets (fig. 4). Leman's designs were truly exceptional, woven in vivid hues and brocaded with exotic, brightly coloured flowers. They also successfully channelled a cultural moment, with some designs inspired by Dutch still-life painting, and brocaded with plant varieties that were being propagated on the lowlands of Europe. At the very apex of this complex industry were the master weavers: superstars like Peter Lekeux, who attracted national attention and wealthy clients. The scale and sophistication of the Spitalfields weaving industry simply added to the special cache of London, this burgeoning city of makers.

By the 1730s, not only was Spitalfields silk famous, but many silk-practitioners themselves had become lauded and sought after. One of the most influential was Anna Maria Garthwaite, who created more than a thousand designs for drawloom-woven silks over three prolific decades. Designed by Garthwaite in 1744, this oyster-coloured satin is brocaded with sprays of flowers in coloured silks, including roses, morning glory and auricula. Originally made into a gown in the mid-eighteenth century when the silk pattern was at the height of fashion, it was later altered and reused (fig. 5). The flowers are painstakingly observed, and even today you can appreciate their detailed, botanical accuracy and aesthetic brilliance. It is an Enlightenment statement, created as the ideas of new taxonomies and classifications of the natural world were being formulated, in the aftermath of the failed Jacobite Risings, as a more confident, outward-looking Britain was evolving.[3] It speaks both to the moment and of powerful globalizing forces, combining native roses with Southern European auricula and morning glory, which would have originated in East Asia: the spoils of an outwardly focused nation, but set against a luxurious gold background to suggest optimism, hope and confidence. Garthwaite seems to want to jolt us with her skill, to shock us with her creative brilliance. Although not a Huguenot herself, she was part of the sector they seeded and must have known her local market, influenced by a Calvinist affinity for the natural world. Like so many of the East End's migrant communities, the Huguenots, when faced with such profound challenges, were determined not just to survive but to audaciously recalibrate people's understanding of living – to create celebrations of natural wonders while gifting the inhabitants of London exquisitely made garments that protected them from the harshness and cold of the city.

Although these eighteenth-century makers would be replaced by subsequent waves of migrants, and although

5.

ANNA GARTHWAITE (1690–1763)

Woman's silk gown (detail), 1745–50.
Ivory damask brocaded in
coloured silk threads

6.

RAHEMUR RAHMAN (b. 1990)

Detail of ensemble (jacket and trousers) from 'Collection 3 – Children of the Rag Trade', 2020/21 the grand houses they had raised would spiral down through multiple cycles of disrepair, the area would continue over the centuries to be a place of refuge and attract creative communities. At the turn of the millennium, the houses around Brick Lane that had been built and once inhabited by Huguenot weavers would begin to be acquired by artists like Jake and Dinos Chapman and Chris Ofili, who themselves would join such long-term residents as Gilbert and George. And a generation on, East London continues to produce these stories. Today, journeymen weavers have been replaced by piece-workers – thousands of British Asians of Bangladeshi or Pakistani descent who, like their forerunners, support the vast base of the contemporary-fashion production pyramid by making affordable clothes. Many work for internationally acclaimed fashion labels, but do so from their homes. They form an extensive, invisible, un-unionized workforce, paid by the garment, often with scant job security or benefits.

The textile artist Rahemur Rahman, born to migrant Bangladeshi parents in East London in 1990, has worked for some of the world's most successful fashion brands. He grew up around Brick Lane, the same streets on which Anna Maria Garthwaite made her name, acquiring similar skills, but a quarter of a millennium later. Both his parents work in fashion: his father in a garment factory, his mother as a piece-worker. Rahman has followed in their footsteps, but his work tells the hidden stories of making and of sacrifice; it is an acknowledgment of the challenges and contributions of a labour force that creates affordable clothing for the biggest brands. Like Garthwaite, Rahman's work is born of contemporary global politics and migration – but also of maintaining connections to the warmth of his cultural heritage. After working in Paris for Louis Vuitton, he returned to London to create his own label and focus on issues of design ecology, supply chains and making practices. This suit evokes textiles conceived in Europe, manufactured in East Africa and then sold across the Global South (fig. 6). It reminds us that the same patterns of exploitation have repeated themselves over centuries; how, from Garthwaite to John Galliano, generations of immigrant London textile and fashion designers have used creative practice as an arena for otherwise hidden voices.

For the post-independence migrants who arrived in London from ex-colonies in the Global South, warmth took on another connotation. For them, warmth could conjure memory and romance. One of the most successful but poignant bodies of work that draws on those themes was created by the textile artist Althea McNish. Born in Trinidad in 1924, McNish would join a generation of West African and Caribbean migrants building new lives in London in the 1950s. She had demonstrated great creative talent in a range of disciplines from a young age, but it was while attending London's art schools that her talent began to blossom into something extraordinary. McNish found a place as part of a post-war explosion of radical graphic expression. Under the tutelage of Scottish artist Eduardo Paolozzi, she chose textiles as her discipline; but her painterly style afforded her fabric designs the weight and gravitas of fine art. Inspired by the botanicals and warm, vivid colours of the Caribbean, McNish's designs not only spoke of her heritage, but also told stories with the power to touch us all.

McNish was commissioned to make ranges for Dior and Liberty, and would even receive commissions from Queen Elizabeth II. These were designs of another time, simultaneously nostalgic and shockingly new – every pattern she conceived was graphically compelling, yet she audaciously constricted herself to perversely narrow palettes. McNish shared much with Anna Maria Garthwaite: inspired by the natural world, she would capture it with great botanical accuracy; she also shared Garthwaite's intellectual and technical flair. She would often leave aspects of the mechanics of her print-making processes evident in the finished work, to remind us of the hand and method of the maker. She was not afraid to evoke a sense of cultural history through complex, ghostly mis-registrations of layers of colour in her prints, deployed to suggest a sense of fragility. These were textiles that brought to mind brittle old frames of film, flickering and stuttering in a camera gate, casting multiple possible realities, all playing out simultaneously. And although she evoked far-away places in her imagery, her priority was to explore internal emotional landscapes that we could all recognize, as well as suggest a shared warmth. McNish's great legacy is a well of exquisitely intimate, fleeting moments from other people's pasts – blurred family photos, old scratched records, memories of half-forgotten places – that seem somehow to belong to us all. It is a body of work that navigates human warmth and belonging, left to us by a brilliant narrative artist (fig. 7).

Although the practice of each of these artists was the product of complex, varied histories, they created work that is underwritten by a compelling universality. In their own particular way, they each produced a Union Jack; they all created distilled celebrations of warmth and cultural complexity that we might identify with and be drawn to. Perhaps, ultimately, they were looking for safe spaces, for warmth – and, in so doing, they created sanctuaries for us all.

7. ALTHEA MCNISH (1924–2020)
OPPOSITE TOP: *Golden Harvest*, Hull Traders, Lancashire, England, 1959. Screen-printed heavy cotton satin furnishing fabric
OPPOSITE BOTTOM: *Trinidad*, Heal's, London, England, 1960. Printed cotton furnishing fabric

ADEBAYO OKE-LAWAL (b. 1990) FOR ORANGE CULTURE

Ensemble of blouse and matching trousers,
'Flower Boy' collection, Autumn/Winter 2020. Printed cotton

Oke-Lawal's 2020 'Flower Boy' collection reframes derogatory remarks he received as a young boy into a celebratory challenge to Nigeria's culture of hyper-masculinity. Printed with flamboyant and colourful hibiscus flowers, reminiscent of wax-resist àdìrẹ prints, on soft, lightweight fabric, this ensemble was designed with a fluid and inclusive approach to gender. The cut and drape of the fabric is representative of Orange Culture's 'universal silhouette', which combines the masculine and the feminine as well as West African and tailored fashions. Reclaiming the joy and warmth of bright hues, and allowing for softness and sensuality, Orange Culture's approach to menswear represents, and allows for the inhabitation of, diverse, global masculinities.

Health

Starting with the outbreak of plague in Europe in the seventeenth century, this chapter examines how design responds to the spread of disease in imaginative, sometimes beautiful ways – from the use of the pomander to the many religious objects and reliquaries said to possess miraculous curative properties beyond the psychosomatic. It concludes by examining the creative responses to the Covid-19 pandemic, including the making of masks, textiles and clothing. Touching on the relationship between art, design and science, it also looks at the many ways in which art can have deeper, wider health outcomes than simply helping us to improve our mood.

On 14 September 1665, the diarist and politician Samuel Pepys added a sobering entry to his journal. He described a walk through a number of London neighbourhoods during which he came to the terrifying realization that illness and death had assumed absolute dominion. He describes plague striking with exquisitely perverse prejudice: taking single family members, or cutting a swathe through whole neighbourhoods, working its way along streets, but occasionally leaving lone homes or isolated, mourning individuals untouched. More than seven thousand Londoners died of bubonic plague that September week. It must have been truly terrifying. The symptoms – fever, sores and vomiting – wove their way across the city with a sadistic deliberation, selecting victims with no evident pattern, but being utterly ruthless when they struck, leaving mourning, scared and devastated communities in their wake.

Pepys rewrote his will, set his papers in order and began to chew tobacco, which was thought to have prophylactic properties. And as a pall of incapacitating terror fell across the city, he wrote: 'nobody but poor wretches in the streets', 'no boats upon the River', 'fires burning in the street', to cleanse the atmosphere, and 'little noise heard day or night but tolling of bells', which accompanied the constant funerals. 'I am come almost to think nothing of it.'[4]

Attempts were made to isolate the infected, but there was simply no effective healthcare-shaped safety net.

There were no epidemiologists, no hygienists, no vaccine programmes; there were no truly effective treatments, no meaningful defence, no real understanding of what was befalling London. And where there *was* a coordinated response, it seemed only to strengthen the feeling of helplessness by having little or no impact. But then, what could be done against this ineffable, unrelenting, ruthless killer that seemed to prey with deliberate delectation upon communities? Over the course of 1665, London authorities recorded 68,596 deaths, but the actual total probably surpassed 100,000 people, more than 15 per cent of London's population. And plague took young and old, wealthy and poor, the previously fit and healthy; no one was immune.

London was not the only place that suffered. Plague was rampaging across Europe, with outbreaks recorded in most of the continent's major cities; and those not directly affected by the epidemic would have had to deal with the wider economic and social crises that followed. Plague raged through Cologne and Amsterdam, then worked its way through France and along the Mediterranean coast. Although little seemed to stop or even slow its passage, observers noticed that wherever there were bad smells there seemed to be higher concentrations of deaths.

Thomas Aquinas, the thirteenth-century scholar, had famously stated that cleanliness is next to godliness. Aquinas argued that god is evident in order, beauty, well-being and hygiene. But London in the 1600s, although one of the world's great commercial centres, was a chaotic place. It was a city that had emerged as a result of little planning or municipal coordination, and during the most intense months of the epidemic, it filled with the sick, the dying and the already dead. Sewage and stagnant water filled the city's gutters and ditches as plague overcame the city. It must have stunk. And although there were no epidemiologists, it was very apparent that Londoners were dying in their greatest numbers where the stench was most intense.

Nosegays, or small bunches of flowers, had been popular since the medieval period as a means of counteracting the smells of everyday London life. In the sixteenth century, John Gerard, the celebrated herbalist, recommended violet, lavender and sweet marjoram, but by the seventeenth century the aromatic cocktails deployed against plague had become much more sophisticated. This was not just about perfume being adopted to disguise foul odours; rather, it was inspired by the thought that fragrance, beauty and aesthetic intervention could be used as an effective barrier against the spread of the pox.

Among the horror and devastation of the plague that ravaged Europe in the seventeenth century, the adoption of exquisitely crafted pomanders became understandably popular. It did not hurt that they resembled thuribles, used in Catholic masses and Freemasonic ritual to decant plumes of incense and perfume at the culmination of ceremonies. Pomanders share that affecting ecclesiastical

8.
POMANDER, 1600–10
Silver, 6 cm (height)

aura. Usually the size and shape of a walnut, they commonly comprise a number of parts, including a bowl or a series of perforated containers to hold the aromatic ingredients. These internal receptacles would be housed within highly decorated silver-gilt cases.

This is a seventeenth-century Dutch pomander (fig. 8). The Netherlands were as affected by plague as England: Amsterdam lost about 10 per cent of its population, some 50,000 people, between 1667 and 1669. Well used and well loved, this pomander would have been suspended from a chain around the neck, to protect its owner. The perforated outer silver-gilt shell is intricately decorated with repeated leaf motifs. The leaf decorations were likely chosen to mirror the contents of the container. The bowl would have been filled with aromatic mixes – herbs, cloves, cinnamon and perhaps ambergris (the solidified vomit of a whale with a waxy consistency that could preserve other ingredients). But part of the efficacy of these objects was their sheer beauty, and a belief in the Aquinas doctrine of beauty – of order being somehow divine and beauty offering a little protective presence in life. And those that believed in the effectiveness of these pomanders really did believe. There were plague reports of thieves who would break into the homes of the recently deceased to steal their possessions, reassured that they would be protected from the plague by the use of a pomander.

There are many cultures in which objects such as sculptures, garments, reliquaries or pieces of jewelry are believed to confer good health and offer protection from sickness. There are Catholic shrines and artefacts that are said to have played miraculous, ongoing roles in people's lives. There are Songhai masquerades in which exquisitely adorned dancers become conduits to metaphysical powers that can shift material reality and be deployed to protect health and aid well-being. For these West African communities, the design of the masquerade costumes is critical to their effectiveness. Across the Muslim world, there are traditions of talismanic objects that stave off ill-health. These might be amulets containing holy verses, carried to offer their owner prophylactic protection from sickness. They might be garments like this shirt inscribed with verses from the Qur'an (fig. 9). It is half a millennium old – but its sweat stains and signs of wear offer a visceral insight into the life of its owner. It is the kind of garment that was worn next to the skin, beneath battle dress or by the infirm, worn to create a tangible connection with its wearer. The owner may have calculated that armour might protect them from an arrow, or from a blow, but this shirt might work on a level of deeper metaphysical causalities to alleviate the very possibility that they might fall victim to a weapon, or succumb to sickness. The vital component of this garment's efficacy (like the religious reliquaries of Christianity) is the spiritual investment of its owner. Without belief, this garment would be simply a beautiful thing.

9.

TALISMANIC SHIRT, *C.* 15TH–16TH CENTURY

Woven cotton, inscribed and painted in ink and gold paint, 64 × 103 cm

These are not baseless superstitions, and art need not possess miraculous properties to have a role in healthcare. Across the history of art and design, objects have played many significant roles in safeguarding our health; and in the twenty-first century, although not as explicitly, the belief that beauty can make a difference to well-being is a quietly accepted aspect of most of our lives. Indeed, recent studies have shown how art can reduce stress, how proximity to beautiful things can increase immunity; that visually considered environments can help improve heart function and lower risk of mental illness.[5] The benefit of being in the presence of beautiful things is real.[6] And it is perhaps at times of great existential crisis that we see this most vividly.

Between 2020 and 2021, even with the deployment of vaccination and quarantine programmes, more than half a billion people contracted Covid-19, with more than 7 million of those dying from the disease.[7] And the emotional fatigue that accompanied the pandemic created its own mental health challenges. With the closure of museums, theatres and concert venues, people began to crave art. Over the course of the first year of the outbreak, one in five people increased their arts engagement, and one in eight increased the amount of arts broadcasting they watched.[8] People naturally longed for the arts as part of an unconscious programme of mental self-medication. A report funded by Arts Council England, 'The Role of the Arts during the COVID-19 Pandemic', noted that

10.

LARA HAILEY (b. 1975)

Sewn Antidote, 2020. Quilt of organdie on canvas backing with 90 applied roundels in different techniques, one further roundel on reverse, 195 × 195 cm

'Arts engagement helped people use certain psychological strategies for coping and emotion regulation, including distraction techniques, social connection with others, learning new skills and engaging the mind, and self-reflection or emotional connection with oneself,' and 'that people overtly recognized the physical health, mental health and wellbeing benefits of home-based arts and cultural activities and pursued them for these reasons'.[9] These conclusions seemed to reflect what the makers of those seventeenth-century pomanders recognized: that beauty matters to our well-being. The arts not only enrich our lives but can also enhance our physical condition including heart health, and may even lower our risk of developing certain types of heart disease.[10]

The artists, designers and makers who worked through the pandemic seemed to recognize this too. Lara Hailey is an artist who has worked in a variety of media, but has been particularly effective in creating collaborative quilts. In 2020, in response to the pandemic, she decided to craft a solution. In *Sewn Antidote*, Hailey borrowed from the long history of quilt making to create a cathartic banner (fig. 10). As she put it, she was 'interested in documenting social history through collaborative stitch projects and how the therapeutic benefits of stitching with a shared aim can create wellbeing and connection in these times of isolation'.[11] Her response was an affecting quilt, appliquéd with more than ninety roundels, each of which speaks to someone's particular perspective on the many varied impacts of Covid-19. It reminds us not just of traditions of communal making, but also of the isolation that the pandemic exacerbated, and of how communal creative responses might just be the perfect antidote. Such responses were also often joyful. In a video on social media, artist Liv Huffman showcased her own crocheted version of a 2020 JW Anderson patchwork cardigan worn by the singer Harry Styles (fig. 11). It went viral, inspiring thousands of Styles fans to make and share their own ingenious interpretations. Delighted by the DIY response, JW Anderson shared a free downloadable pattern and tutorial for the cardigan. Itself a comforting, colourful object, the cardigan fostered social ties and creative purpose at a time when many suffered through loneliness and the pain of physical separation.

Tellingly, artist Bita Ghezelayagh refers to this mask she made in 2021 as her 'lockdown friend' (fig. 12). The green base fabric of the mask is made of silk velvet, handwoven on a traditional loom in Kashan, Iran. Inspired by an online film about a spider-silk cape from Madagascar that was displayed at the V&A in 2012, Ghezelayagh added an embroidered golden spider crawling across a web that she had silkscreened onto the velvet. The artist identifies spiders as symbols of the cosmos, while the web represents the homes we were trapped in during lockdown. The spider itself, a motif for a universe of possibilities, was a creative collaboration: a crucial connection within the restricted freedom of the pandemic. It was made by

11.

LIV HUFFMAN (b. 1998)

Cardigan (detail), 2021.
Acrylic, wool, crochet

a teacher at the Royal School of Needlework in London, and Ghezelayagh notes that they discussed 'every thread used in making it'.[12]

The global usage of face masks reached a staggering 129 billion per month during the early stages of the pandemic.[13] The vast majority of the masks used in those first months of the outbreak were disposable, and, being made of mixed materials, were difficult to recycle. Designers and artists stepped in to create multi-use, washable face masks that, while more sustainable, also seemed to address people's wish to wear masks that reflected their personalities, that might be uplifting or inspiring – perhaps, like the pomander, simply through proximity – as well as protecting the wearer and those around them from the spread of disease. Equally, buyers supported and celebrated artisans during the pandemic by purchasing these more considered objects, such as the face masks made by Esam Ali of Cairo's Street of the Tentmakers. Using an appliqué technique known as *khayamiya*, this particular example has been decorated with traditional designs extracted from large-scale wall-hangings or soft furnishings (fig. 13).

To return, then, to Samuel Pepys's diary and the entry written in mid-September 1665, at the very height of the Great Plague, when the mortality rates were at their most extreme, and after Pepys had returned home after a long day out walking. He pauses momentarily to reflect that the day has left him utterly overwhelmed by what he has

12.
BITA GHEZELAYAGH (b. 1966)
Golden Spider mask, 2021. Screen-printed silk velvet, 15 × 17.5 cm (excl. ties)

13.

ESAM ALI (b. 20TH CENTURY)

Mask, 2021. Cotton with cotton appliqué designs, 10 × 20 cm

encountered. Not just the proximity to so much death, but also the recognition of the fragility of so much of what we depend upon. And so he ends that day's entry with a few revealing and touching words: 'I put off the thoughts of sadness as much as I can, and the rather to keep my wife in good heart and family also.'[14] I believe that Pepys's loving sentiment holds a clue to one of the keys to well-being and the benefits of the arts. During the trauma of the pandemic, people needed things to offer them 'good heart'. In the middle of so much death, upset and disruption, they wanted some respite and joy, perhaps even a little beauty. It was in this regard that small things such as an artist-designed face mask might just have offered them a modicum of 'good heart'. The very smallness of such gestures made them all the more profound. Design is not just about beauty or entertainment, or even function. The scale of these aesthetic acts of defiance speaks to the indefatigability of the human spirit when faced with a seemingly insurmountable challenge and very few options. As so many of the post-pandemic reports concluded, in times of great challenge the arts become even more important; they can build confidence, positivity and a sense of connection, while creative engagement can reduce feelings of loneliness and anxiety. But even ambient exposure to culture can inspire, lift one's spirits and make the heart swell. Although these feelings can be hard to measure and quantify, their importance when we experience them can be unlike anything else.

DESIGNED BY ISINNOVA
AND MANUFACTURED BY OLDRATI, 2020

Snorkelling mask fitted with Charlotte valve;
injection-moulded plastic

In 2020, hospitals in northern Italy were overcome by the number of patients suffering from Covid-19. One of the many challenges was the scarcity of respiratory equipment. Renato Favero, a retired doctor, contacted Isinnova with the idea of repurposing a full-face snorkelling mask into a CPAP (continuous positive airway pressure) mask. In response, Isinnova created the Charlotte valve in collaboration with sports retailer Decathlon to fit to an off-the-shelf snorkelling mask. Once there was a working model, the design files for the core components were made freely available online. The design has been downloaded more than 2 million times, and repurposed masks have been used in many countries around the world.

0-10

SCENT CASE, 1600–1700

Silver, 2.5 cm (diameter)

This seventeenth-century scent case takes the form of a snail, perhaps inspired by the creature's ability to withdraw inside its shell for safety. Pierced on one side to release the perfume, this hinged case opens to reveal an engraved skull on one side and a butterfly on the other. Worn suspended from a chain about the neck, or from a belt or girdle, scent containers like this one may have been thought to embody amuletic properties, able to ward off the pestilent foul odours.

Sleep

Sleep is central to human life, not just as a practical necessity but also as a way of understanding death and as a gateway to the creativity and spirituality of dreams. This is the story of the pursuit of sleep (and status), from a nineteenth-century colonial campaign bed to a transparent orange acrylic box developed in 1990s Britain that proposes to protect the sleeper from harmful emissions – a reflection, perhaps, of our dwindling amounts of sleep and the fetishization of its pursuit. This chapter explores how we use sleep as a spiritual metaphor, from Aboriginal 'dreamings' from Australia to the deeply affecting late nineteenth-century fashion for photographing the recently deceased.

14.
TWO AFRICAN MEN CARRY
A EUROPEAN MAN IN A HAMMOCK, 1884
Wood and paint, 45 × 112 × 30 cm

It is 1884 in Berlin, and Western European nations have begun negotiating how they will carve up, colonize and exploit the remaining independent areas of the African continent and consolidate what they claim already to hold. Some eight thousand miles away, in Congo, a Bembe artist turns his focus towards one of the many early European traders travelling in the region (fig. 14). Carved from a single block of wood, it is the work of a highly skilled artist with forensic and merciless flair for observation and parody. Although it was made for the European market, it is not a flattering piece. It is tragic and comic. The African porters are lost, and the European traveller is on the verge of sleep, in a state of semi-consciousness in the last, fleeting seconds before he drifts off. They stop – the confused man at the front points ahead, the bemused man at the back gazes after him, tears running down his cheeks. The European was never in charge, always a passenger. In his lap lies a rifle, and between his legs a sleeping dog: everything about him suggests torpor, malaise, inaction. All are tied together, all condemned by fate; the figure at the front seems to know where they might be going but the figure behind understands how lost they all are. It might be funny, but while it serves as a commentary on imperialism, it is also an uneasy essay on sleep, on the moment when we are carried into unconsciousness, when we topple and fall, when we relinquish control and drop: a moment that is both terrifying and comforting. We slip, or are conveyed into a realm beyond our comprehension or direction, never certain of where we might go – or if, indeed, we will return.

Although we spend as much as a third of our lives asleep, sleep itself remains something of a mystery. We know it is important in giving our bodies and minds time to repair and rest, that it offers us the opportunity to set down memory and process trauma, that it is the time when the brain expels toxins and the body regulates our metabolism. And yet aspects of sleep remain an enigma. It is the giving up of control, the loss of consciousness, the immersion into a vivid other-world somehow created by you, informed by your experiences, sometimes rational and coherent, but at other times chaotic and strange, and with the potential to be more terrifying than almost anything that most of us will encounter in life. Sleep is a realm where we can surprise, disgust and delight ourselves, where we can learn about our hidden thoughts, our buried desires and motivations, things that can be illuminating or terrifying. Sleep is a state that strangely occupies some of the same territory as art, reflecting alternative perspectives on situations, pushing ideas further than might be comfortable, and occasionally serving to inspire or lift our spirits.

In the 1880s, as the outcomes of the Berlin Conference were beginning to be felt across the British Empire, a number of new light infantry companies were being formed to better police British colonial territories. The Argyll and Sutherland Highlanders would be deployed variously to the Boer War, the Irish War of Independence, Ceylon (now Sri Lanka) and India. It was in India, in the early twentieth century, where the aptly named James William Stratton Gurney, an officer in the Argyll and Sutherland Highlanders and a lecturer at the Engineering College in Roorkee, near Delhi, would commission a camp bed (fig. 15). It is a humble piece of furniture, but also quite a stately one. In palette, pattern and materials, it is very similar to the hammock bedding of the sleepy European in the Bembe carving. Made by one of Gurney's Indian students, it was designed to fit into a travelling cabinet and move with the British officer when he escaped the summer heat of Delhi and retreated to his residence in the foothills of the Himalayas. Officers would travel light, carrying clothes and collapsible furniture, like this bed. Although it was designed to be light and mobile, it was also conceived to be comfortable and beautiful. The woven surface of the bed is not only patterned but also perfectly tensioned – taut enough to offer support, but also slack enough to give comfort. For a piece of mobile military equipment, it is almost unnecessarily over-considered, with its tapered edges and its intricately designed and woven surface; it has been made to remind us of the importance of sleep and to be a fitting vessel to carry us into the realm of unconsciousness.

While artists from Rubens to Shona soapstone carvers, from Picasso to Chinese ceramic pillow-makers, have captured the *act* of sleeping, there are also artists who have sought to look beyond the act to uncover its mysteries. Published in 1899, Sigmund Freud's *Interpretation of Dreams* is the work in which he first introduces Europeans to the notion of the unconscious – a sphere of escape, of secrets, of truths. It is this vision of sleep as a hidden psychological hinterland that has also intrigued many artists across the world. The possibility of sleep or dreams being a realm of escape is something that the Aboriginal peoples of Australia have spent millennia considering. The 'in-between', the semi-lucid time that the Bembe artist captures, is also the realm of Aboriginal creative focus, out of which has come a set of maps and tools for navigating that mental twilight between consciousness and sleep, between memory and imagination, between history and the present. No Aboriginal languages have a word for time, and (rather than turning history into a science, in which we seek out corroborating evidence to place on a timeline) Aboriginal peoples accept that our relationship to the past is fluid, that we can deploy our imagination, our consciousness, our dreams to enter the connective space between now and the past or the future. They have built an exquisite body of visual practice to map and navigate this dream terrain.

Susie Bootja Bootja Napangarti was an Aboriginal artist from Western Australia who explored this subject matter through her work. Her 2002 screen print *Kaningarra* straddles time; it is a re-imagining, a dreaming of a moment when a couple meet (fig. 16). It captures the landscape as it might be viewed by a bird, the area as it was affected by human presence, the boomerang-shaped impressions their bodies left on the ground, and the undulations across the terrain and the hills on the horizon. It is a landscape painting, a map, a diagram, but one that charts time and imagination as well as place and its energy. Aboriginal peoples believe in networks of Song Lines, or dreaming tracks, that criss-cross landscapes and connect important

15.

CAMPAIGN BED, EARLY 20TH CENTURY

Collapsible campaign bed with turned and lacquered legs, strung with coloured wool, 50 × 70 × 140 cm

16.

SUSIE BOOTJA BOOTJA NAPANGARTI (*C*. 1935–2003)

Kaningarra, 2002. Screen print, 56 × 76 cm

locations. These areas could be traversed and navigated by songs alone, sometimes by singing and evoking the locations in a memory or dream, or while walking the route, when the song could be deployed as an aural map – a guide that would correspond to the spirit and energy of the landscape.

The Faraday Chair is the work of Dunne & Raby, two British conceptual designers (fig. 17). Its name is a reference to the Faraday cage, a structure – named in turn after the scientist Michael Faraday – created to resist and offer protection from electro-magnetic fields. Here, Dunne & Raby have made an item of furniture with a function beyond holding an unconscious being. Although it looks like a flotation tank, it is in many ways concerned with attaining a state of being similar to traditional Aboriginal dream-states. *The Faraday Chair* was created with the aim of blocking out all forms of electrical energy – radio waves, Wi-Fi signals, emissions from everyday appliances – so that we might be left to feel the stillness of the Earth, to rest, reflect, sleep, dream and connect. The hope was that within the still isolation of *The Faraday Chair* we might be left with the unadulterated purity of our dreams. Although the work is non-functional and cannot take measurements – it is a conceptual piece – its aesthetic is one we might recognize from visits to hospitals or clinics. *The Faraday Chair* seems to infer the importance of an unconscious state and an aspiration to navigate, measure and record its mysteries.

The literary and visual arts movement known as Surrealism came into being after the First World War. It was driven by a wish to explore the unconscious mind, to draw its mysteries out into the world. Its champions, such as Salvador Dalí and René Magritte, were creative superstars within their own lifetimes. But some of the most potent investigations of our dreams were created by more reluctant, reclusive, introverted artists not directly associated with the movement, or who even preceded it. Eugène Atget took up photography in the 1880s with no desire to be famous, to make a fortune, or to disrupt his discipline. He sought instead to quietly capture the world about him.

Starting in the late 1890s, Atget embarked on a lifelong project to document old Paris before it was changed by modernization. But there was something about his images, his subjects, something about the way he went about his work, that intrigued the Surrealists who encountered him. It was as if he had inadvertently captured the atmosphere of dreams – as though we were being offered privileged, private access to that unconscious realm through his work. Here, personal perspectives, dream visions that we should not be able to share, were suddenly made tangible, present and public. Atget took photographs of Parisian streets, buildings and interiors (fig. 18). They are strange images, slightly haunting, ethereal, ghostly; they are not unsettling, but you do feel wrong-footed, almost like looking at the world through a sepia-tinted

17.
DUNNE & RABY
The Faraday Chair, 1995. Welded steel frame, acrylic, silicon, cotton pillow, 71.8 × 125 × 72 cm

18.

EUGÈNE ATGET (1857–1927)

Intérieur de Monsieur T., négociant, rue Montaigne (Interior of Mr T., merchant, Montaigne Street), 1910; printed 1978. Albumen print, 28.5 × 24 cm mirror. It is a mirror that somehow does not reflect our presence: we have become the ghosts. And maybe at the heart of this vision is a confrontation of the fear that is integral to sleep, navigating a line that seems as though it might place us in worrying proximity to death.

The relationship between death and sleep was a constant area of exploration for many in the late nineteenth century. Following the invention of the daguerreotype – the first publicly and commercially available photographic medium – its early practitioners realized that this medium was not like other art forms; it captured a perfect visual facsimile of a moment in time on a sheet of highly polished and silvered copper. With the high rates of infant mortality in the period, those with the financial means and access began to think that this new technology might have a role in mitigating the finality of death. Photography allowed for the possibility not just of capturing a lasting image of a recently deceased child, but of posing them as if they had just drifted off to sleep (fig. 19). Such images tempted the viewer to imagine that the subject might be about to wake up. They spoke not only to the idea of the relationship between death and sleep, but also to the thought that if these two states are connected, then perhaps the camera could capture time and might even be able to defy it.

Sleep might be mysterious, but maybe that is part of its wonder. It is perhaps within the realm of dreams that our early human ancestors discovered the potential to

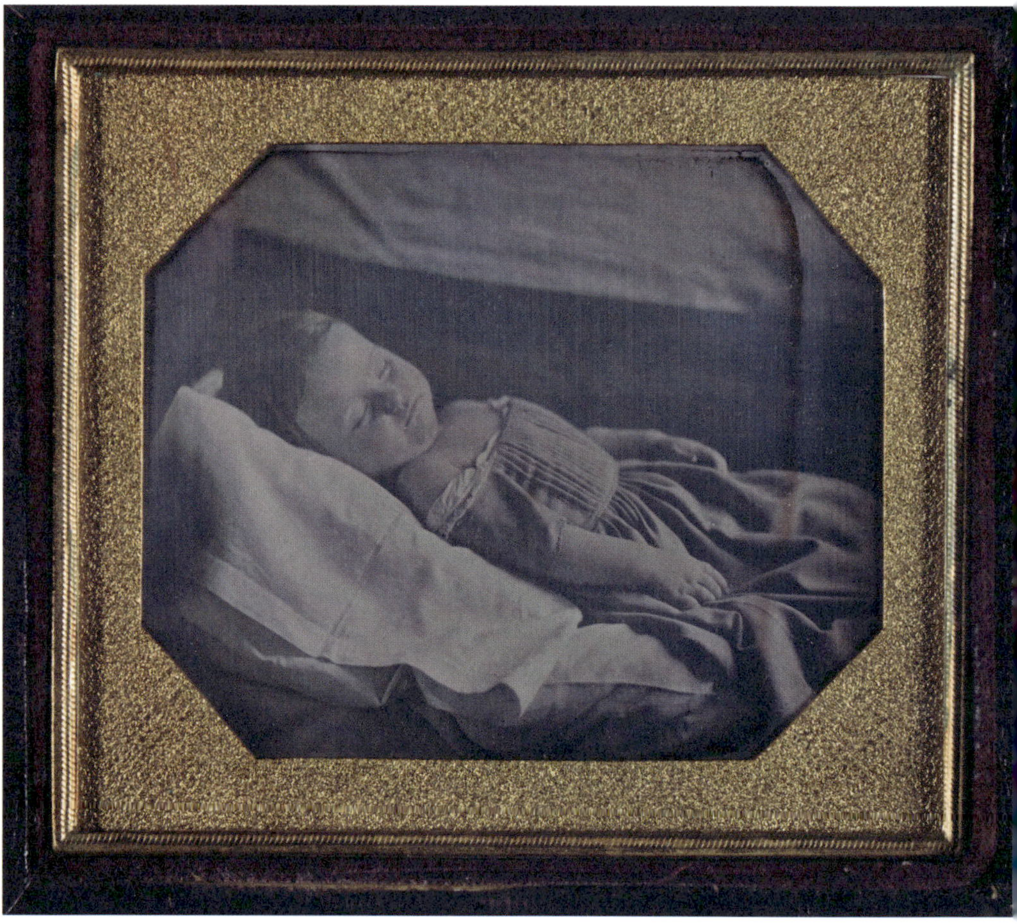

19.

DECEASED YOUNG GIRL, *c.* 1845–55

Daguerreotype, 9.5 × 8.3 cm (incl. case)

craft narrative, to create fictive landscapes, to make art. But dreams also suggest possibility; they imply that life could be different, and that we could be the protagonist in shaping change. Artists have recognized that powerful potential lies within our own unconscious and have found the tools to mine and navigate it. And so perhaps it is easy to understand why artists have found sleep a constant source of inspiration, whether that might be the capturing of the act of sleep itself, or finding ways to capture that journey into unconsciousness, or even to capture, chart and replicate what might lie on the other side.

ANTONIO CANOVA (1757–1822) AND WORKSHOP

Sleeping Nymph, 1821–24. Marble, 194.3 cm (length)

A leading exponent of the Neoclassical style, Italian sculptor Antonio Canova is known for the grace and idealized beauty of his marble figures, as well as his remarkable ability to bring warmth and sensuality to cold, white stone. Inspired by the sculptures of ancient Greece and Rome, the composition of *Sleeping Nymph* was informed by the classical *Sleeping Hermaphrodite* (*c.* 100–150 AD). Left unfinished at Canova's death in 1822, *Sleeping Nymph* is one of a group of the sculptor's later works that depict the reclining form; here, the nymph, a personification of nature, lies naked on her front on top of a rock partially covered with drapery.

VISHNU RECLINING ON THE SERPENT SHESHA, LATE 18TH TO EARLY 19TH CENTURY

Cast copper alloy, 14.5 cm (width)

In this small bronze, the reclining figure of the Hindu deity Vishnu, the protector or preserver of the universe, rests on the coils of the serpent Shesha. Asleep in between the cosmic cycles of creation and destruction, Vishnu is supported by the great snake's boundless body, which represents eternity as well as embodying stability and order amid change.

Creativity

Creativity has been with us since humans first made marks, but at certain times in history there have been periods of particular artistic ferment and transition. Taking as its starting point a 1926 backdrop by Natalia Goncharova for Diaghilev's production of Stravinsky's *Firebird*, this chapter explores a moment that was not just a high-water mark for ballet and the creative arts, but also represented the beginning of a significant change in cultural politics in Europe, a moment that appeared to offer hope for those who had sat in the margins.

The twentieth century did not begin with the passing of the nineteenth. The stubborn, lumbering Victorian certainties dug in. The manners, the mores, the unspoken understandings that had underwritten the era of colonial consolidation held firm across Europe. The vast enlightenment intellectual order simply refused to budge. But then, in 1905, over a short, seismic passage of months, the inner gearing of culture in the Global North began to shift – and the new century arrived in earnest. It was not just a change in the world as it was, but a shift in the very nature of our understanding of what creativity might be. In 1905, Freud published his *Three Essays on the Theory of Sexuality* and Einstein his first paper on relativity, while the first members of the Bloomsbury Group began to meet at Vanessa Bell's Friday Club in London. In 1906 Henry Ford took over as president of Ford Motor Company and began to shape his vision for the Model T, the first mass-market car – the efficiency of his assembly lines inspiring a new functional and industrial aesthetic. Cubism was created by Pablo Picasso and Georges Braque in Paris, and in 1907 Picasso finished *Les Demoiselles d'Avignon*, perhaps the most influential single piece of art of the twentieth century. In the same year, the brilliant Russian impresario Sergei Diaghilev delighted Paris by staging a panoramic, five-concert series of different types of Russian music at the Grand Opera. In 1909, the Italian poet Filippo Tommaso Marinetti published his *Manifesto of Futurism*. Roger Fry then shocked the art world with his hugely influential London show of Post-Impressionism in 1910 – the year in which, according to Virginia Woolf, 'human character changed'. In 1913, the Armory Show in New York would introduce the work of the European avant-garde to the United States and become a catalyst for American modernism; in Europe, meanwhile, Stravinsky's *Le Sacre du Printemps* would cause the audience at the Théâtre des Champs-Elysée in Paris to riot. Across a range of creative disciplines, a ferocious cascade of innovation seemed to erupt, and the momentum and nature of change seemed simply to quicken and intensify.

Each creative shift appeared to stand in some way on the shoulders of the last; each offered new insights on freedom and possibility; each cemented a further fundamental reconfiguration of the world in favour of you and me. Suddenly, once marginal, voiceless communities seemed to matter in ways that had previously seemed impossible. While Einstein, Freud and Ford tore up the accepted blueprint of the mechanics of our future, a hidden battle began for our cultural destiny. Who would compose the fanfare for the common man, write the clarion call for the voiceless? Who would paint our banners and build the totems to celebrate the hidden heroes?

The classic percolation downwards of high ideas was being challenged, replaced by the rise of new creative voices. It was a wind of change that was whipped up in the great industrial heartlands of the Global North and then infected the psyche of the rural poor. Through the music

20.

DESIGNED BY PABLO PICASSO (1881–1973), PAINTED BY PRINCE ALEXANDER SCHERVASHIDZE (1867–1968)

Front cloth for *Le Train Bleu*, 1924. Oil on canvas, 1 × 1.1 m of Harlem, the union newspapers of Detroit, the novels of the American plains, the politics of St Petersburg, the painting of Paris and the poetry of London, modernity was born. Creativity has been with us since humanity gained self-awareness, but there have been periods of particular artistic ferment and transition throughout history – moments when art does not just reflect the ambient mood, but becomes one of a number of catalytic forces driving change.

In 1909, Diaghilev's *Saison Russe* in Paris dazzled audiences with a combined spectacle of innovative music, choreography, dance and design. Officially formed in 1911, the Ballets Russes would revolutionize ballet; through collaborations with influential modern artists such as Léon Bakst, Natalia Goncharova, Henri Matisse and Picasso (figs 20 and 21), it would also incorporate and, in turn, influence the most important artistic developments of the twentieth century, leading to an enduring legacy in art, theatre, fashion and interior design. Singularly able to recognize and bring together pioneering artists from across a variety of fields, Diaghilev was a man who thrived on risk, on thrilling audiences with innovation and invention. He commissioned young, groundbreaking composers such as Igor Stravinsky, Sergei Prokofiev and Erik Satie, composers who embraced unusual sources of inspiration, sought to be less formal and structured, and took risks in their visual style and musical form. Appreciative of the fashion for Russian arts, and for ballet in particular –

the Polovtsian Dances performed from the opera *Prince Igor* in the 1909 season having received great acclaim – Diaghilev was inspired to commission a new, all-Russian ballet for European audiences. At the outset of the 1910 season, he wrote: 'I need a ballet, and a Russian one – the first Russian ballet, since there is no such thing – there is Russian opera, Russian symphony, Russian songs, Russian dance, Russian rhythm – but no Russian ballet.'[15] His quest was informed by a desire to create something radical and ambitious, something that spoke to this moment in history. For this, Diaghilev placed his faith in Stravinsky, a young acolyte of Nikolai Rimsky-Korsakov. Diaghilev paired his protégé composer with rising-star choreographer Michel Fokine and the trustworthy stage designer Alexander Golovine. In Stravinsky he believed he had found something truly special, worthy of the best support. 'Mark him well,' Diaghilev noted, 'he is a man on the eve of celebrity.'[16]

Stravinsky, like so many of his contemporaries, sensed the cultural change on the wind, a challenging of conventional thinking by drawing inspiration from unconventional sources. Where Freud and Picasso had leant on African art as their muse, Stravinsky looked to Russian folk music to catalyse his creative thinking. He worked at lightning speed, completing the score for Diaghilev's new Russian ballet in under six months. *The Firebird* felt like a chance to reflect something of the revolutionary tang that hung in the air. It told the story of the downfall of a powerful, evil ogre through the intervention of a mythical,

21.

PABLO PICASSO (1881–1973)

Costume design for the Chinese Conjuror from *Parade*, 1917. Pen and ink on paper fire-feathered bird. It spoke to the moment, it drew from the past – but it was ultimately about the future.

First performed on 25 June 1910, *The Firebird* was the triumph its creators had hoped it might be, a huge success with both critics and audiences. Stravinsky later recalled: 'the first night audience at the Paris opera glittered indeed … I sat in Diaghilev's box where at intermissions a stream of celebrities, artists, dowagers, writers, balletomanes appeared … I was called to the stage to bow at the conclusion and was recalled several times.'[17] Its themes of powerful, beautiful forces administering karmic justice felt cathartically prescient.

Over the next decade, Europe dissolved into war and revolution. Millions lost their lives in the first truly global conflict – and revolution would overturn the established order of Russia (Stravinsky's and Diaghilev's home). For many, the compendium of threats felt existential; the demands of these vast theatres of conflict would tax the world in unprecedented ways, pulling people from every region into complex mobilizations to support supply chains or join the legions of personnel risking their lives in action. But the gathering of so many young people from so many areas of the world gave rise to a wide range of unexpected outcomes. Europe became a crucible for new ideas – writing, creative thinking and music. Ragtime became the sound of the 'rear areas', places behind the front line where soldiers could take temporary respite from the heat of battle. This new music, born of the period's irrepressible defiance, touched a political nerve. In 1918, Stravinsky, the great cultural sponge, premiered *The Soldier's Tal*e, an exquisite, miniature jewel of a piece based on a Russian folk tale, influenced by ragtime and jazz. *The Soldier's Tale* told the story of a soldier-musician meeting and being tempted by the devil. But its ultimate message was one of the trenches, of sacrifice, of the nobility of the marginalized and forgotten.

At the end of the First World War, Stravinsky returned to *The Firebird*. The ballet's themes seemed to have a different resonance after the loss of so much life, in such appalling circumstances. His new *Firebird* would draw on the post-revolutionary moment of his native Russia; it would take something from the tragedy of the Great War; it would acknowledge the new heroes while also looking back at Russian history, its people, its folklore and its deep reservoir of unresolved pain. For this, Stravinsky and Diaghilev would turn to one of the great Russian avant-garde artists and creative campaigners of the time, Natalia Goncharova, asking her to redesign *The Firebird* in 1926.

Goncharova was a carefully considered choice for the design of sets, costumes and the invention of a visual world. She had first collaborated with Diaghilev in 1914, accepting an invitation to design sets and costumes for his 'opera-ballet' production of Rimsky-Korsakov's opera *The Golden Cockerel* (fig. 22), and then, a couple of years later, for Stravinsky's ballet-cantata *The Wedding* (*Les Noces*). She was brilliant in the revolutionary way that Stravinsky

22.

NATALIA GONCHAROVA (1881–1962)

Preliminary design for backcloth for *The Golden Cockerel*, 1914. Watercolour on paper, 56.5 × 78.3 cm was: she was a leader in the Russian avant-garde, a pioneer of the art movements Cubo-Futurism, Rayonism and Neo-Primitivism, and worked across so many styles and media that the writer Ilia Zdanevich described her prodigious output as *vschestvo*, or 'everythingism'.[18] She seemed like a woman unencumbered by the weight of the moment, almost as if she hailed from a future age.

It also helped that Goncharova was utterly fearless. Her practice was groundbreaking in all the right, but contentious, ways. As Picasso was looking to traditional Iberian carving, before his adoption of Africa as an inspirational muse, Goncharova sought inspiration in Russian folk art, combining such things as the religious icon, peasant embroidery and *lubok* woodcut prints with the innovations of modernist artistic styles. Her work was labelled primitivist, or folk (labels that sometimes came with a pejorative taint to them), and yet Picasso and Goncharova both sought to make statements about the possibilities for modernizing, for making the world more equitable. Goncharova's inclusion of subjects with lower social status, including Russian Jews, was controversial, while her interpretation of religious themes offended the Orthodox canon and was censored. Her treatment of the nude, particularly the female nude, even led to Goncharova being charged and tried with displaying 'corrupting pictures' in 1910.

The most provocative element of her work at the time may simply have been that it was produced by a woman.

Goncharova had suffered profound gender discrimination as a young artist, even being denied her diploma at the completion of her degree at the Moscow Institute of Painting, Sculpture and Architecture. But Goncharova was a force of nature who simply would not be cowed; she would turn those obstacles into points of inspiration. She would define herself as a world artist, an internationalist who identified with neglected, marginal voices from wherever they came. She subsequently dedicated much of her energy to driving change – and possessed the important ability of making herself heard. She was a founding member of the Donkey's Tail, Russia's most notoriously uncompromising and radical artistic group, which seemed to thrive on controversy, deploying sometimes shocking creative techniques to convey ideas. The group sensed that long-overdue change was on the cards, and where it could not deliver the freedoms and equity it craved, it would draw attention to the fact. To promote the opening of her first major retrospective in Russia in 1913 – the first of its kind for any member of the Russian avant-garde – Goncharova orchestrated a parade of Futurist 'body' art through the streets of Moscow for which she and her fellow artists had hieroglyphic patterns painted on their faces. She was a deeply unconventional but charismatic figure who allowed little to stand in her way.

Although Goncharova was radical and ambitious, the post-war financial constraints forced everyone working on the new production of *The Firebird* to tighten the budgetary strings. But Goncharova thought carefully about where she should be utterly uncompromising in her vision and make a powerful aesthetic, perhaps even a political impact. Her most astounding intervention would be a vast new stately backcloth for the second and final scene – the moment when the evil ogre's spell is broken, his palace disappears, the once-dead are reanimated and there is celebration. As the backdrop to this dramatic climax, Goncharova created a truly monumental panorama: a view not just across a Russian skyline, but also across Russia's recent history (fig. 23). It was a temporal mirror within which the past and the future appeared the same – in which the minarets and onion domes of Russia's history appeared as its destiny. For those post-war and post-revolution émigrés who joined the audience at London's Lyceum Theatre on 26 November 1926, the narrative arc of *The Firebird* must have felt like a communal exhalation of long-pent-up air, an exorcizing of ghosts – the spell had been broken. They would have recognized 'old' Russia in the city of minarets and onion-domed churches within a kremlin wall. They must have seen the city they loved but had left in the painted rooftops, the silhouettes of the old centres of administration and state. They might have recalled the traditional folk art of their childhoods in the pared-back graphic brushwork. They may have felt a warm wave of nostalgia, or maybe the sadness in the loss that this history represented. But they probably also felt the hope, the sense of a new dawn over that horizon.

This was a work that spoke to the Russian diaspora, to posterity, to the post-war, post-revolution moment – it was a ferocious, passionate, beautiful roar of hope. When there seemed little to feel optimistic about, this felt audaciously needed and important. It is said that when Rachmaninov listened to *The Firebird* for the very first time and witnessed the dramatic final movement, he was moved to remark, 'Great God! What a work of genius this is! This is true Russia!'

And perhaps the discovery of important truths was also Natalia Goncharova's ultimate ambition. She had seemed to spend a significant amount of her life focused on considerations beyond the creative; she wanted justice, to reach out to the marginalized, to support unfashionable causes and make a difference – and perhaps sought to use the creative realm to catalyse discourse. The century had begun by asking testing questions about the past, seeking new ways of being. And maybe in drawing on the rebirth of Russia as a point of inspiration, Goncharova sought a symbolic rebirth for us all. She wanted the world to feel the optimism of the moment – to look out across and beyond the horizon. Her backdrop of Russian architectural iconography spoke to more than Russia; this was a message to a bruised and battered global generation that had staggered through the First World War, and done so at great cost. This was their firebird, their salvation, their romantic past, and their hope for the future. And the conduit for that hope was creativity.

23.

NATALIA GONCHAROVA (1881–1962)

Backcloth for *The Firebird*, 1926. Painted canvas, 1 × 1.6 m

CHRISTIAN OVONLEN (b. 1987)

Pineapple Cloak and *Rainbow Wolf* hangings from the *Ballet Russes* series, 2021. Hand-painted and printed silk hangings, each 301 × 102 cm

The vibrancy of these hanging textiles echoes the energy of the stage performances from which Christian Ovonlen, a London-based graphic artist, has drawn inspiration. Created over a period of nine months in 2021, Ovonlen's *Ballet Russes* series depicts a vivid sensory experience: music, costume, dramatic lighting and scenography metamorphosed into luxuriously hand-painted and hand-dyed silks. Starting with pastel drawings, Ovonlen then developed a method for translating his detailed mark-making and bold designs into large-scale silk hangings.

Shelter

Although one of the first human needs to come to mind, the provision of secure shelter has always been a challenge. This chapter focuses initially on the social-housing explosion of the post-First World War period, with the Frankfurt kitchen – widely celebrated both in Germany and abroad, and becoming a prototype for all built-in kitchens – embodying a modernist ideal of efficiency, rationality and hygiene. It then follows the journey of London's Robin Hood Gardens from the idealistic dream of its design to its disillusion, demolition and recuperation.

There is a passage towards the beginning of Daniel Defoe's 1719 novel *Robinson Crusoe* in which the newly shipwrecked castaway adds a poignant entry to his journal: 'I walked about the shore almost all day, to find out a place to fix my habitation, greatly concerned to secure myself from any attack in the night, either from wild beasts or men. Towards night, I fixed upon a proper place, under a rock, and marked out a semicircle for my encampment; which I resolved to strengthen with a work, wall, or fortification, made of double piles, lined within with cables, and without with turf.' Crusoe's drive to find shelter is understandably immediate, primal. But almost as fundamental are several connected emotions. First, a desire for order, and then two conflicting but affecting sentiments: a fear of others, and (as we discover when he comes across a footprint on the beach) a deep longing for others too. Home is the symbolic resolution of these impulses, a protected environment in which we can feel safe with those we care about.

Although one of the most basic and critical human needs, the provision of secure shelter has not always been easy. In almost every human society, our relationship to shelter has been complex, fraught, often deeply contested, and sometimes very political. Shelter is rarely just about protection from the elements, but part of a range of ways in which we demonstrate and understand our hierarchies of intimacy; how we show who is really important to us, who sits within our family and friendship circle, our community, our peer group – and who does not. There are few other things on which we place so much financial and emotional value, and that says a great deal about who we are. Our homes, and where and how we seek shelter, are deeply connected to identity and heritage. Homes are often a proxy for wealth, for social status and a mechanism through which an array of assumptions can be made about our histories, politics and culture. And perhaps because of the unique place our homes occupy in our lives, the design and look and feel of them have been of special importance to us since our distant ancestors painted the walls of their caves by firelight.

In the years that followed the First World War, a new generation of architects emerged across the globe. They shared those same Robinson Crusoe-like impulses: how to make good places to live where people might feel safe and at ease. The aftermath of the war hung over Europe, but it offered the chance to recast the world, to reimagine how we might live better together. The new politics, the new moment, demanded new kinds of spaces. And a new cohort of architects stepped up to answer the call – initially from Europe and the Americas, and then, a generation later, with decolonization, from across the Global South. Some of the most passionate and articulate architects to first embrace these challenges and opportunities were Walter Gropius and Ludwig Mies van der Rohe in Germany, and Charles-Édouard Jeanneret (who would later assume the name Le Corbusier) in France. Together they created a manifesto for change through architecture, seeking to build spaces based on an egalitarian ambition. It was an architectural set of aspirations that would be eagerly adopted, adapted and nuanced for different regions and parts of the world; and while each iteration was unique, they were all connected by an aspiration to emancipate people from sub-standard and unremarkable architecture. Looking at the fussy, often untidy and even dangerous architecture they had grown up with, Gropius, Mies and Le Corbusier wanted to make radical change. They wanted to craft clean, light-filled homes and workspaces for everyone. They looked at the sprawling, poorly built and designed residential areas of the working classes, at houses often constructed cheek-by-jowl, with poor sanitary provision. They looked at the often dull, uniform houses of the middle classes and at the pampered luxury of the owner classes with their highly decorated rooms and their pared-back, often gloomy beneath-stairs service spaces. They looked and they wanted something else. They sought innovations in materials to shift the very nature of a domestic environment. They used plate glass, cast iron and reinforced concrete, changing possibilities of volume, cost and scale. These innovations were married with simplified concrete spaces with curtain walls that made domestic environments more flexible, and electric lighting and new wall finishes that freshened spaces. They sought to remove ornamentation and excessive decorative flourishes and rely on the integrity and beauty of materials. It was a revelation, unlike anything that had preceded it. It was Modern.

One of the most interesting architects to emerge in the period following the First World War was Margarete 'Grete' Schütte-Lihotzky. A recent graduate, Schütte-Lihotzky had studied at the lauded University of Applied Arts in Vienna. Even before her degree, she had garnered a favourable reputation, championed by Gustav Klimt, and she joined a faculty that boasted luminaries such as the artist and writer Oskar Kokoschka. Schütte-Lihotzky came from an influential, liberal family whose members seemed to effortlessly dominate the creative disciplines. Yet despite such a background, she faced an early obstacle, later recalling: 'Nobody could imagine hiring a woman to build a house in 1916.'[19] But the post-war Vienna into which she graduated, in 1919, was a different world, and she was ambitious. Like her whole generation, Schütte-Lihotzky must have felt the intellectual gear-shift. Following the end of the First World War and the implosion of the Austro-Hungarian empire, Vienna seemed hungry for change. The socialist government began a programme of social housing, within which Schütte-Lihotzky quickly found a role. She was a strong supporter of the left-leaning government and discovered an environment rich with opportunities for challenging the architectural old guard.

Schütte-Lihotzky could see that many Viennese were struggling in out-of-date and unsafe domestic spaces. Quoting Heinrich Zille, the German caricaturist, she said:

'You can kill a person with an apartment just as well as with an axe.'[20] Informed by the work of Frederick Winslow Taylor, an American mechanical engineer who pioneered ways to improve industrial efficiency, tightening and optimizing manufacturing processes, Schütte-Lihotzky sought to apply his principles to the domestic environment – to offer women in particular the benefits of this revolutionary thinking. Her work and ideas began to attract attention, and in 1926 she received an invitation from Ernst May, a highly influential German urban planner. May saw a place for Schütte-Lihotzky, delivering components of his new social-housing scheme in Frankfurt. Under May, Frankfurt – perhaps more than any other European city – had been captivated by modernist thinking. All new municipal architecture was modernist, and the city was markedly and quickly transforming. May wanted a kitchen design that would fit with his ambition to create a modern, safe, clean domestic space in which people could be productive.

It was a timely project. In the United States, the psychologist Lillian Evelyn Gilbreth had just begun to apply time-and-motion analysis to the idea of the kitchen, optimizing the placement of the critical components of food preparation within a given space. Gilbreth conducted studies into the convenience of the conventional kitchen, analysing and reconsidering safety, efficiency and hygiene. It was revolutionary. It treated women and domestic spaces seriously. Schütte-Lihotzky wanted to

24.
MARGARETE (GRETE) SCHÜTTE-LIHOTZKY (1897–2000)
Frankfurt kitchen, designed 1926–27

push these ideas further, to realize them practically, to create safer, cleaner and more efficient domestic spaces that would be pleasurable to be in – and she wanted to do so at scale. What Schütte-Lihotzky and May conceived in Frankfurt went beyond an evolution of the kitchen. Schütte-Lihotzky changed the paradigm of domestic food preparation, shifting it from the dangerous, nineteenth-century kitchen into a light, clean, airy space in which people would seek to spend time.

Schütte-Lihotzky and May's team would conceive a design that would be replicated with subtle variations more than ten thousand times in social housing across Frankfurt. It turned the kitchen into a scientific domestic workspace, a laboratory (fig. 24). This was a kitchen that boasted glazed cupboard space, sealed painted surfaces that could be easily wiped clean, areas for preparation, washing and serving, storage of various kinds, and integrated components such as a drop-down table. It simply made sense from the moment you entered. It was not just a more efficient kitchen; it also showed respect to women and domestic work, alleviated domestic chores and put its users first. The idea of the kitchen being the hub of the home – the kitchen as an inviting, emotionally intelligent environment – had been realized.

Although Schütte-Lihotzky took on the challenge of changing the domestic environment to help women, she was a feminist who had little or no interest in cooking. She later said, 'If I'd known people would do nothing but talk about the damn kitchen, I wouldn't have invented it.'[21] Ultimately, she did not see it as just a tool; to her, the kitchen was an important mechanism in negotiating overdue respect for people and labour. Of course, this was not a panacea to wider issues of gender politics, but it helped to turn an arena of inefficiency and drudgery into a space where we might feel at ease.

These ideas and aspirations would inform innovations in architectural design for much of the twentieth century.

Many subsequent generations of architects were both inspired by early modernism and found ways to iterate or push back against it. Colonialism would carry its principles out across the Global South, where, in the post-war period, it would be finessed and particularized, adapted and reconstituted through the lenses of its users.

One of the most striking manifestations of this process of adaptation was the work of British architects Alison and Peter Smithson. The Smithsons would create a body of social housing within the mid-century architectural movement known as Brutalism. The movement's name was derived from the term *beton brut*, or 'raw concrete', coined by Le Corbusier, who had wanted to make a case for the beauty of unfinished concrete within the living environment. Sometimes, *beton brut* could have a silk-smooth finish, so smooth that it resembled polished plaster or alabaster. But it could also be shuttered with planks of un-planed wood to leave the rough grain set into the outer surface of the concrete. At its best, in its most pared-back, uncompromising, starkest form, *beton brut* could be breathtakingly beautiful. And so, it would be deployed in both high-end, luxurious architectural projects and vast urban social-housing schemes.

Like Le Corbusier's designs, the Smithsons' living environments were driven by uncompromising ideas of form, and concrete was the most flexible material with which to achieve these ideas. The couple would be celebrated for their vast, pre-cast concrete buildings or complexes that could hold hundreds of separate dwellings. The Smithsons saw their buildings as canvases on which communities might craft new ways of collaborating and living together. They hoped that their blocks, their 'streets in the sky', would become places where their residents' domestic dreams might be realized: concrete balconies wide enough for several people to walk and socialize, for children to play, extended towards the centre of the site, overlooking the communal garden at the project's heart.

In common with the work of Ernst May, the social-housing complexes designed by the Smithsons were, in their original manifestation, radical advances on what traditional social housing offered. Schemes such as Robin Hood Gardens in Poplar, East London, were celebrated when they opened in the 1970s. The apartments that made up the scheme were single-floor units or maisonettes with wide balconies. Although they borrowed from nineteenth-century conventions, such as alcoves and an intimate cosiness, in many ways they followed the patterns of pre-war modernist developments, with clean, light spaces. However, as the London docks were decommissioned, there was a profound shift in the local economy: by the 1980s, the area was stricken by poverty, and the urban structures suffered as a result. As new businesses and developments began to redefine East London, bringing with them social conflict and economic disparity, such estates began increasingly to show their age. In contrast to the sought-after communal areas that the

25.

ALISON SMITHSON (1928–1993)

AND PETER SMITHSON (1923–2003)

Robin Hood Gardens, Poplar, London, 1972 (completed)

26.

DO HO SUH (b. 1962)

Robin Hood Gardens, Woolmore Street, London E14 0HG, 2018.
Three-channel video piece (still)

Smithsons dreamed of, the shared spaces of Robin Hood Gardens were vulnerable to neglect, vandalism and crime – and the concrete aged surprisingly badly: the word 'brutal' seemed no longer applicable to just the concrete finishes. By 2013, the scheme was scheduled for demolition to make way for a new regeneration project.

On the eve of its destruction in 2017, the V&A acquired a three-storey section of each of the scheme's façades and the interior fittings of two of the flats (fig. 25). It also commissioned the artist Do Ho Suh, whose practice centres on the idea of home as both a physical structure and a lived experience, to create a new work (fig. 26). Inspired by the architecture, interiors and people of Robin Hood Gardens, Suh's resulting panoramic film used time-lapse photography, drone footage, 3D scanning and photogrammetry to create a visual journey in which the camera pans through and around the building to reflect the 'energy, history, life and memory that has accumulated there'.[22] In addition, artist Jessie Brennan's four graphite drawings, *A Fall of Ordinariness and Light* (2014), are an elegiac tribute to Robin Hood Gardens and the inhabitants affected by circumstances beyond their control, each drawing individually subtitled with terms taken from the compulsory purchase order issued by the London Borough of Tower Hamlets in 2013: 'The Order Land', 'The Scheme', 'The Enabling Power' and 'The Justification' (fig. 27). Brennan's work captured the shift in attitude towards this kind of response to the social-housing need.

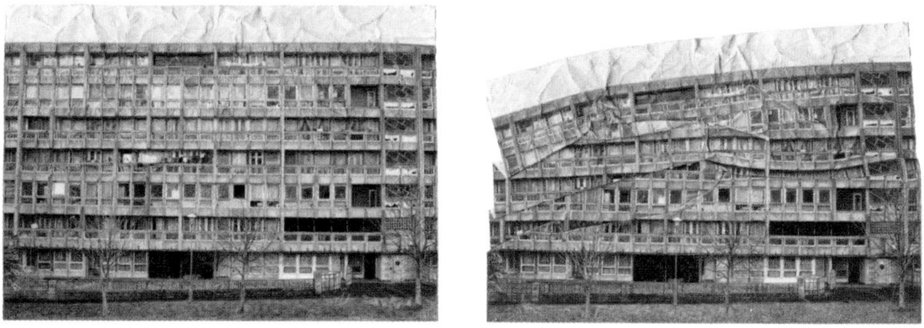

27.
JESSIE BRENNAN (b. 1982)
A Fall of Ordinariness and Light, 2014.
Pencil on paper, each 50 × 64 cm

When Robinson Crusoe saw that footprint in the sand, he was both thrilled and alarmed by the thought of sharing his beach with others. The powerful needs that Defoe identified – of desiring shelter, of seeking control and order in one's home – are timeless. We need spaces that feel good to be in, that are designed in ways that make us feel safe, comfortable and content. These are qualities that Schütte-Lihotzky sought to integrate into her own designs: she made her kitchens utterly compelling. Although she said she disliked domesticity, she understood how homes worked; she knew that good kitchens were the comforting heart of those Frankfurt homes. She wanted to shine a spotlight on those spaces, to foreground women's needs and their often gendered work. It was a creative but also a political act.

In some ways, Schütte-Lihotzky's ambitions were similar to those of the Smithsons. They too hoped that a layer

of magic might be absorbed into the fabric of their spaces through their users' presence; they imagined that people would gradually humanize and soften Robin Hood Gardens simply by living there. The Smithsons and the residents of their Poplar scheme sadly found that those shared spaces did not organically evolve into deeply successful communal areas. Where there was any neglect in the shared areas of the estate, it would metastasize and become a foothold for crime, vandalism and other anti-social behaviour. This led over time to a deep communal disenchantment. And at the root of the residents' complaints were the architectural features of Robin Hood Gardens. In 2018, just half a century after the first residents moved in, the process of demolition began, and the streets in the sky came tumbling down. The dream was over. And yet the legacies of modernist architecture – the finishes, the architectural sector's enduring aspiration for communal living, the global iterations on modernist themes, the chucking-out of chintz, the modernist knock-offs – seem only to grow stronger.

SONIA BOYCE (b. 1962)

Umbrella made for *Portable Fabric Shelters* at London Printworks Trust, 1995. Screenprint on an umbrella, 90 cm (diameter)

In 1994, London Printworks Trust commissioned a group of artists to make work for an exhibition entitled *Portable Fabric Shelters*. The theme was global migration, and the status of refugees and the homeless. Sonia Boyce made a number of works for the exhibition, including blankets, a tent and an umbrella. The last of these spoke to the complex issues of refuge, its edges fringed with pairs of closed eyes, offering a space from which to share another's perspective. A form of mobile and potentially shared shelter, an umbrella can keep strangers at arm's length but also provide cover for those we choose to share it with.

TOM HUNTER (b. 1965)

Woman Reading a Possession Order, 1997.
Dye destruction print, 60 × 40.8 cm

This image, from Tom Hunter's photographic series of squatter communities in East London, focuses our attention on a woman and child in the light of a window. The careful composition and framing of the image are deliberately reminiscent of a seventeenth-century painting by Johannes Vermeer, *Girl Reading a Letter at an Open Window* (1657–59). Depicting a young mother reading an eviction notice in a sympathetic, positive light, this image became part of a successful dialogue with the local council in which houses were saved from demolition.

Property

The need to collect, to possess, to own, to have dominion over things and even people has been one of the most potent and corrupting of human drives. The history of our varied and interconnected notions of property, ownership and control has been one of the most fraught aspects of human history. From the possession of precious treasures and nations to people themselves, and the authorship and regulation of both cultural and personal narratives, we follow the intertwined and competing notions of property that affect a culture in the years that precede and follow the creation of a colony.

In many ways, this box might be considered a modest object (fig. 28). It could fit in the palm of an average adult hand. It is made from brass – a not hugely valuable metal – and its surface is decorated simply. It is not the bright, polished brass of a trumpet; its patina suggests that it has been well loved and used. It was made in the late nineteenth century in the Gold Coast, a region in West Africa that is now modern-day Ghana. The box was designed to hold gold dust, the metal that both made and destroyed the culture that created it. And like so many objects in the V&A, it might appear simple, but it is part of a complex and important story of ownership and property.

In 1814, a young British writer, Thomas Bowdich, was offered a life-changing assignment by the African Company of Merchants – the chance to meet a whale. Bowdich was commissioned to initiate contact with one of the most charismatic of the West African monarchs: Osei Bonsu (1779–1824), king of the Asante, or the Asantehene.[23] The hope was that the Asante might agree to the establishment of a British trading post on the West African coast, from where the fledgling African Company of Merchants might acquire and export gold and slaves. Bonsu's reputation preceded him: his wealth and his wisdom were well documented. Rumours about the sophistication and cosmopolitan nature of his court spread out along the West African trade routes to tease and beguile his rivals and trading partners. Bonsu was known as a brilliant tactician, a formidable intellect and a lover of history.

28.
BOX, LATE 19TH CENTURY
Cast brass, 2.4 × 7.5 × 3.6 cm

He understood that knowledge of history was a powerful tool and recognized that heritage might be a useful social bond for a young state. He understood the potential of good history to underwrite legal systems, how the right stories might orientate, guide and build shared values. And he would talk at court about the political value of history, of the sheer reputational heft that could be engendered through well-deployed shared knowledge. Perhaps because of his unique reputation, Bonsu became known by many who spent time with him as 'the Whale', not just because of the scale and influence of his court, but also because of his extensive knowledge of its history – and his great fondness for publicly delving into its depths.

During Bonsu's reign, the Asante empire had grown significantly in both influence and scale. It expanded east and west to incorporate the gold-rich forested regions, north into the Sahel, and south towards the strategically important coastline. Indeed, at the height of Bonsu's Asante empire, the southerly extent was marked by Cape Coast, one of the most significant slave ports of the era. Cape Coast Castle was a vast industrial slaving complex that fed the transatlantic slave trade. It was one of many similar, fortified coastal buildings through which millions of people would be corralled and traded. Although this was a sophisticated state that seemed to value dignity and humanity, its economy was underwritten by slavery, by the commodification of its fellow citizens. And similarly, although the British had outlawed the buying and selling of enslaved people within its empire, although they proclaimed it an age of enlightenment, although they were crafting a new national discourse on rights, they continued to benefit from the slave trade, and to work to control, colonize, corral and commodify whole regions of the African continent and its peoples.

Bowdich knew that Osei Bonsu was no ordinary figure, that the Asante kingdom was no average state, that this was no simple assignment. There were other gold-rich states in West Africa, but even by comparison with its nearest rivals, the Gold Coast produced fantastic amounts of very high-quality gold. In just a couple of generations, the state had used its wealth to build great armies and more than double the size of its territories. The more gold they mined, the bigger the armies they could muster; the bigger the military force, the greater the economic influence, and the more significant the territories they could control. They turned their state into an ever-expanding, voracious machine that swallowed neighbouring kingdoms and accrued greater wealth while turning those they conquered to the campaign of further conquest.

Bonsu was an unusual leader. While he drove the expansion of his empire with an unrelenting will, he was also interested in culture and intellectual pursuits, attracting diplomats, thinkers and academics from across North and West Africa to his court. He surrounded himself with writers and philosophers, the intellectual innovators and regional superstars of the age. Bowdich described early nineteenth-century Asante as a dynamic hive of activity, a nation with the economic buoyancy and strategic guile to attract entrepreneurial talent from across West Africa and beyond. In his published journal, Bowdich recalled a lavish yam festival, attended by hundreds of local and foreign dignitaries. At the centre of the celebration sat the Asantehene – Osei Bonsu, 'the Whale' – wearing beautifully worked gold and exquisite cloths, presiding over his family, his court and his friends and allies. It is a magnificent scene of a confident, prosperous culture with an expansive, engaged view of the world. At its heart, however, this meeting was about gold, and Bonsu controlled the entire supply chain – from the most productive gold mines to the jewellers, the smithing guilds and the networks of traders. It made him unimaginably wealthy and incomparably powerful. And as you might imagine, his treasury and private collection boasted some of the finest pieces of gold ever cast using the lost-wax process.

Into the bosom of this extraordinary kingdom came Thomas Bowdich, negotiating his passage. And the Asante kingdom was all he imagined and more. But there was an implicit race afoot. While Bowdich was describing the Asante court as other travel writers might have described the great courts of Venice or Constantinople, the German philosopher Hegel was crafting his great encyclopaedic record of humankind – within which, with no empirical knowledge, he cast Africa in a very different light. '[As] far as history goes back,' he wrote, '[Africa] has remained, for all purposes of connection with the rest of the world, shut up; it is the gold-land compressed within itself – the land of childhood, which lying beyond the day of self-conscious history, is enveloped in the dark mantle of night.'[24] Like many of his contemporaries, Hegel believed that as Europe was entering an age of reason, the naturally blessed African continent was being left behind, locked in a culture-free state resembling Europe's dark and distant past. This was a view that offered Europe's fledgling imperial programme in Africa a tacit mandate. It gave permission to Europe's traders, many of them more aggressive and gold-hungry than Bowdich, to consider means other than the diplomatic to gain access to Africa's assets. They believed that their presence might be a blessing for this rich, non-Christian region – that this was a continent ripe for the taking. And they knew that whichever European nation built that first substantive relationship with Osei Bonsu would likely yield huge economic advantage (fig. 29).

Bowdich understood the scale of the potential prize. He would have heard about the rich, accessible seams of gold that, according to local lore, would leave glistening nuggets in riverbeds after rain. He may well have seen the exceptional jewelry crafted by Asante smiths, and then carried on camel trains and sold into the great markets of the Middle East and southern Europe – and he must have calculated the astronomical worth of winning this diplomatic prize. This was a real-life El Dorado, a kingdom of

29.

CHARLES SALLANDROUZE DE LAMORNAIX,
AFTER A DESIGN BY JEAN-BAPTISTE AMEDEE COUDER

Africa, 1855. Tapestry woven in wool
and silk on cotton, 290 × 142 cm

gold. And like those mythical golden kingdoms, the mines of 'the Whale', and the markets over which he presided, were so geographically remote to Europeans as to render them almost mystical, magical, supernatural; between them and Europe or the Middle East lay vast oceans, and deserts. But the unattainable nature of these gold-rich states, and the lack of knowledge about them, only made them a more alluring prize.

You can imagine how our beautiful box would have been indispensable. For a trading-class household, gold was more than currency; it was life-blood and cultural signifier. And boxes such as this one would have contained gold in its most accessible and useful form: as dust that could be weighed, exchanged and treasured. Small brass or bronze weights were used to weigh gold dust in all transactions. Often exquisitely crafted themselves, Asante gold weights might resemble court regalia, such as this example in the form of a ceremonial sword, or represent popular proverbs, as in the case of this weight in the form of an antelope (figs 30 and 31). The extended horns are a visual pun on the benefit of hindsight, referring to the Asante saying, 'Had I known my horns were to grow so long, I might not have started'. For a young state, the accrual of gold was one of the ways in which those not belonging to the aristocracy might build wealth, and perhaps a little power. And the Asante understood how to deploy gold, not just as currency but as a medium through which to broker and barter that power. Indeed,

Bowdich was given a gift by the Asantehene of an exquisite gold lute, a symbol of harmony and continuity – of the potential partnership of two great nations. But we must also reconcile that this obviously thoughtful, accomplished Asante state oversaw the capture and supply of hundreds of thousands of people: individuals who were forced into slavery, even in the years after the trade had been outlawed.

Perhaps predictably, within a generation of that Bowdich visit, the Asante state would become one of the wealthiest and most influential in Africa, catalysed by an intercontinental trade in gold, slaves and ideas. However, few foresaw that within the lifetime of many of those present at the yam festival that had welcomed Bowdich to the Gold Coast in 1814, the British influence would strengthen and spread, turning a small defensive foothold on the coast into a burgeoning crown protectorate.

In 1874, the British sent an armed force to lay siege to the Asante capital, Kumasi. The days of Bowdich's subtle diplomacy were over. By the 1870s, Britain had grown very good at this sort of campaign. It was led by Sir Garnet Wolseley, 1st Viscount Wolseley, a veteran of many punitive imperial expeditions. Wolseley was not only a brilliant tactician but also seemed to relish such endeavours. In 1857, when he was part of the British force sent to end the Siege of Lucknow in India, he wrote of his desire to exterminate the 'beastly niggers', to shed 'barrels and barrels of the filth which flows in these niggers' veins'.[25]

30 & 31.
UNKNOWN MAKERS
TOP: Goldweight, late 19th century. Cast brass, 10 × 5.3 × 1.25 cm
BOTTOM: Goldweight, before 1874. Cast brass, 3.2 × 7.6 cm

32 & 33.

UNKNOWN MAKERS

TOP: Ceremonial cap (*denkyemkye*), 19th century.
Antelope hide and gold, 24 × 56 × 21 cm
BOTTOM: Trophy head, 18th or 19th century.
Gold, 20 × 14.5 × 14 cm

In Kumasi, the British had a small, well-trained force, armed with Enfield rifles and Gatling guns, which could fire hundreds of rounds a minute. Within months, they had burned the royal palace to the ground, taken possession of the crown jewels and the state treasury, and forced the abdication of the Asantehene. Among the items taken from Kumasi during that raid were some of the most exquisite examples of West African lost-wax goldsmithing. The sale and dispersal of this incredible inventory of objects was overseen in London by Sir Richard Wallace (founder of the Wallace Collection), who was working on behalf of Garrard & Co., the royal jeweller. It was said to have amazed even the most experienced London art dealers.

From beautifully fashioned gold rings to gold amulets with layers of lace-like filigree and the exquisitely detailed sword of state, it was a dazzling collection that demonstrated skill and experience of the very highest order. Among the many objects that stood out within this extraordinary collection was a richly decorated ceremonial cap known as a *denkyemkye* (fig. 32). It was said to have been worn by senior courtiers at coronations and other major festivals. But perhaps *the* stand-out piece was a life-sized golden head made by an artist of outstanding talent (fig. 33). In what is arguably one of the finest collections of African gold objects ever assembled, this head was exceptional. It was part of a tradition of depicting high-status enemies and would have been attached to a sword of state. This particular head depicts a chief from northern Banda state who was assassinated in the middle of the eighteenth century, and was probably cast soon after the chief's death.

It is tempting to try, just as Richard Wallace did, to calculate the financial value of this collection, but that is probably impossible. The true value of these objects was always beyond financial assessment. They told the story of a nation, and held something of its spirit. The main bulk of the collection would end up in a number of museums in the Global North, including the Fowler Museum at UCLA, the British Museum, the Wallace Collection and the V&A (fig. 34).

A generation after the raid on Kumasi, in a now famous passage of historical events, the British governor of the Gold Coast, Sir Frederick Mitchell Hodgson, demanded that he be given the golden stool of Asante – one of the few truly iconic objects that had survived the British invasion, an object that was said to have descended from the sky at the moment of the nation's founding – so that he might publicly sit on it. This strange request suggests that the colonial administration understood something of the significance of these collections, that they understood that – despite the invasion – they had not truly beaten the Asante people. The British, like the Asante, knew that this was more than a collection of beautiful things, more than examples of exquisite goldsmithing. In many ways, these objects were the manifestation of the spirit of a people, a nation's heritage so deep a whale might

34.

BADGES WORN BY THE 'SOUL WASHER' OF THE ASANTEHENE (KING OF THE ASANTE), BEFORE 1874

Cast gold. TOP: 12 × 13.2 × 2.8 cm

BOTTOM: 9.9 × 9.7 × 1 cm

dive in it and swim; a reservoir of succour and ghosts that might underwrite communities. The British knew that the objects had the power to unite, focus and make sense of a proud nation; that they had the power to convey weight and continuity. They knew that loved and truly iconic objects had the power to anchor history and narrative, to rally and galvanize us into casting hopeful and ambitious eyes towards the future.

The Asante never gave up the golden stool.

Within a handful of years, more than quarter of a million ounces of gold were being exported annually from what were, by then, the richest industrialized mines in the world. With the creation of a British colony at the turn of the twentieth century, gold, manganese, bauxite, diamonds and a variety of other valuable raw materials were being exported on an unprecedented scale. The Gold Coast was a formidable repository of resources for the British Empire, and although Asante dignity was compromised, their resources exploited, their economies yoked and broken, they refused to give up their golden stool – the metaphorical font of the nation, the source point of their history.

It was right, but perhaps overdue, that in 2024, to mark the 150th anniversary of the raid on Kumasi, the British Museum and the V&A loaned back the gold material taken from the Asante palace in 1874. British museums, limited by statute, could not simply 'give' these works, but were imaginative in forging tenable agreements with the Asante royal palace. It was a poignant occasion – a moment to reflect on these difficult histories, on ideas of property and possession, and to perhaps embrace a new beginning.

It could be said that our empty brass box, once a repository of gold dust, is a good metaphor for our story. It is now one of the few nineteenth-century Asante objects to remain in the V&A. It is in many ways a humble object, designed to be used, held, carried, filled – created to be loved. The surface has been decorated to resemble fabric, to suggest one of the many textile traditions that were so valued by West African cultures. Ten knowing pied crows adorn its lid, witnesses to the passage of time – vigilant observers of those who colluded in the enslavement and colonization, of those who collaborated in turning people into property. But they also bore witness to those who stood firm in the face of incredible imperializing forces. Although the box no longer holds its precious contents, the stories, the narratives it has witnessed, persist. Although histories are desperately fragile, when respected they have demonstrated a formidable durability. And perhaps, like so many things that humanity has sought to trade, the box ultimately defies value; maybe it transcends the very nature of exchange itself. Despite its modest nature, it is a deeply valuable object that holds universal, timeless lessons for us all.

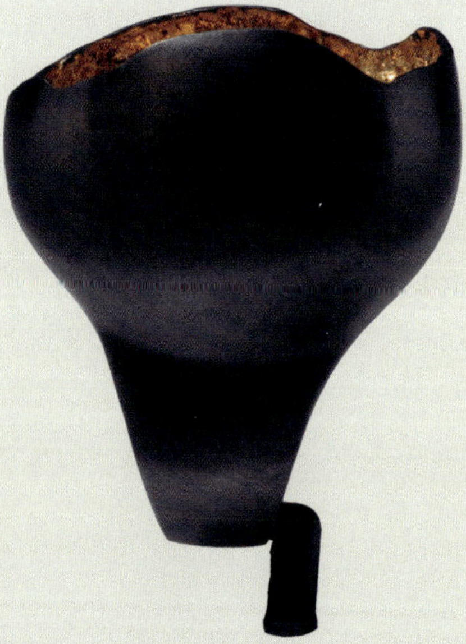

EMEFA COLE (b. 1979)

Ring from the *Vulcan* series, 2012.
Oxidized silver and gold leaf, 4.3 × 3.8 cm

Ghanaian-born artist Emefa Cole has been fascinated since childhood with the treasures that emerge from within the Earth. In her practice, Cole draws from her own heritage and connection to West Africa's tradition of master goldsmiths, and in 2020 she worked with goldsmiths of the Asantehene in Kumasi, Ghana, to learn traditional Asante casting techniques.

Cole's work is often inspired by the forces of nature that are both creative and destructive, such as volcanoes. This ring, from the *Vulcan* series, was initially modelled in wax in one piece before being cast in silver using the lost-wax technique. The dark patination of its smooth, polished exterior contrasts with the rich softness of the gold leaf within. Made in 2012, it was shown at Ghana Fashion and Design Week, Accra, the following year.

HEW LOCKE (b. 1959)

The Prize from *The Rivington Place Portfolio*, published by the Brodsky Center for Innovative Editions, 2006–07. Digital prints with silkscreen, collaged into a 3D structure, with plastic beads and flowers, 76 × 51 cm

This mixed-media collage by Guyanese British sculptor Hew Locke was inspired by a chalice he saw at the V&A. Constructed from cut and woven paper parts, the work incorporates photography, screen-printing, and digital and manual cutting and pasting. The original object is altered to become something gaudy: the images worked into the collage are of kitsch plastic toys and decorations, while the finished piece was embellished with actual plastic flowers and beads. *The Prize* thereby suggests a hollow victory, alluding to both looted treasures and British imperialism of the nineteenth century, as well as the contemporary impact of capitalism and global trade. Perhaps expressing a hope for some kind of cultural recovery from a lust for power and wealth, the satirical phrase 'get well soon' is repeated in the pattern of the work.

Confidence

There are creative declarations that announce a sense of standing in the world, from the Alhambra in Spain to Machu Picchu in Peru, from portrait commissions to street style. When the Torrijos ceiling was commissioned at the end of the fifteenth century, the Castilian aristocracy of Spain was asserting itself. Columbus was preparing for his first transatlantic voyage and the Castilian monarchy was displacing the Nasrid dynasty in the south. This story explores ways that confidence is asserted through design, from personal adornments as compact as a handbag to the encompassing statements of architectural display.

When Italian forces invaded Ethiopia in 1937, they set their minds on more than just winning battles and establishing a colony. Still smarting from the humiliating defeat at the hands of the Ethiopian emperor's army in 1895, when they had to turn on their heels and flee, the Italians on this occasion were taking no chances. This was about asserting confidence and pride. And so, the Italian military attacked Ethiopia with unanswerable force: it dropped 300 tons of mustard gas, a chemical warfare agent intended to blind, flay and compromise lungs; it deployed flame throwers to liquefy skin and eviscerate flesh; it used dundun bullets to smash bones and disable. Many of the Ethiopian soldiers were armed only with spears. A quarter of a million Ethiopian troops were killed in battle, 35,000 people lost their lives in concentration camps, 24,000 were executed after the war – and some 300,000 civilians died in the aftermath. And the Italian forces would go on to loot and pillage and carry away some of the most important symbols of Ethiopian heritage. They did not want only to win; they wanted to humiliate the Ethiopians by taking their land, their dignity, and by robbing them of their cultural heritage and national identity. This was not just the crushing of an empire; the Italians brought about the end of one of the oldest monarchies on Earth and the last independent African nation of the twentieth century. Among the objects plundered from Ethiopia was the obelisk of Axum: a fourth-century, 24-metre-tall, 160-ton, exquisitely decorated stele that was transported and reconstructed to stand in central Rome outside the Ministry of Italian Africa. A once great symbol of pride for the Ethiopian people became a symbol of pride and confidence for the Mussolini government.

Pride is a curious drive, too often attained at the cost of others. For some it is a deadly sin, often achieved just before a fall. Yet its close relative, confidence, is a sentiment around which many of the most marginalized and persecuted have built a positive narrative and a sense of solidarity – and it has been the driver for some powerfully inclusive and affecting creative statements too. Valued by the most oppressed and by some of the most heinous oppressors, confidence is an important cultural driver. The lubricant of identity and creativity, it is a vital component of human life.

The history of the relationship between Africa and Europe has not always been characterized by one-way conquest, slavery, colonialism and exploitation; there were millennia when they saw each other as peers, trading partners and rivals. The medieval European paintings of the Nativity that depict a wealthy and self-assured African-intellectual-nobleman offering gifts to the infant Christ were commentaries on the contemporary interdependent trading geography of Africa, Asia and Europe. The three kings, the three wise men, or Magi, have been a feature of Christian worship since the early medieval period. But the tradition of the Magi themselves, the noble gift-givers who attended the birth of Christ, is derived from the eighth-century Persian priests and astronomers who attended the ancient courts. In the early Middle Ages, as the cost of crusades began to take its toll on Europe, the notion of distant Christian empires as possible allies once again became increasingly attractive, and the three wise noblemen took on a heightened cultural significance. They were given names – Caspar, Melchior and Balthasar – and were said to come from the kingdoms of Tarshish, Sheba and Seba ('Seba' was thought to be an ancient name for Ethiopia). The exotic gifts they carried spoke to the new multi-polar trading opportunities that were redefining the age. Panels like this one spoke to a renewal of confidence, to the crafting of a new sense of cosmopolitan possibility (fig. 35). The younger African king on the far right wears the modish clothing of the period, his youthfulness perhaps a measure of the European view of the relative cultural immaturity of Africa (although maybe, as stories of the fantastical wealth of a prophesied crusading African king began to spread across Europe, this wealthy, wise, youthful figure also represents the future). His jacket, or jerkin, worn over a doublet (which is underneath and not visible), his close-fitting, slashed trunk hose, his square-toed shoes – all were in fashion during the first quarter of the sixteenth century. He is also wearing a fashionable 'Milan bonnet' under his crown.

But pre-colonial Africans exchanged so much more than just precious materials. Many of the most important advances in algebra, astronomy, geometry, calculation,

35.
UNKNOWN MAKER
The Adoration of the Magi, lower part of a rood screen, *c.* 1520.
Oil and gilt on oak, 92 × 116 × 14 cm

prime numbers and algorithmic theory would evolve as a series of intercontinental dialogues that might take generations to resolve.

In the eighth century, North Africans were the majority of the invading Muslim population that settled on the Iberian Peninsula, carrying their thinking, their traditions and their values with them. Over the next 500 years, a series of Islamic administrations, or caliphates, ran and culturally dominated the region. They were not the benign wise men of the Nativity, but they did bring gifts. Al-Andalus, as Islamic Iberia was known in Arabic, became a dynamic hybrid of Islamic, Christian, European, Middle Eastern and North African influences. It was a period of stunning invention in a range of creative disciplines. One of the disciplines that experienced the most spectacular innovation was architecture, where the conceptual and aesthetic perspectives of North Africa were widely adopted across the region, especially in the twelfth century, when al-Andalus was ruled successively by two dynasties of North African origin: the Almoravids and Almohads.

The North Africans had spent millennia developing technologies to cool buildings, channelling fresh air through precisely orientated apertures and fretworked screens deep into their domestic spaces – and engineering sophisticated irrigation systems to carry water across arid environments to supply farms and ornamental gardens in regions that might otherwise have been uninhabitable. They had lived in style and luxury in places where life seemed unlikely. More than just being effective, these systems became sought-after, fashionable aesthetic embellishments that changed southern European architecture. Perhaps the most compelling surviving example is the Alhambra in Granada, where an exquisite palace complex serves as the backdrop to a suite of otherworldly Islamic gardens. Construction of the palace began in the thirteenth century under the rule of the first Nasrid emir; such was its complexity that it would take three hundred years to complete. Islamic cultures generally did not depict the human body in their art and decoration, instead taking their visual inspiration from patterns inspired by nature, geometry, calculus and astronomy. These patterns are evident in areas across the palace and its gardens, carved into friezes, cut into latticed screens, and inlaid and painted onto ceilings. Islamic influence touched many areas of, and had a lasting impact on, Iberian architecture and decoration. And the Alhambra is one of the most remarkable and celebrated suites of buildings in the world. Later, towards the end of the fifteenth century, it would become the royal court of the then ruling Catholic monarchs, Ferdinand and Isabella.

The late fifteenth century was a period of growing confidence in Spain. King Ferdinand and Queen Isabella had stabilized their now Catholic nation and were displacing the Nasrid dynasty in the south, widening their influence by brokering new trading relationships

36.

UNKNOWN MAKERS

Torrijos ceiling, *c.* 1490
Pine wood, carved, painted and gilded;
with modern plaster of Paris panels

and sponsoring New World exploration. It was a time for a new a political elite, for figures such as the influential courtiers Gutierre de Cárdenas and his wife, Teresa Enríquez, to negotiate their way into the political limelight. Cárdenas was a brilliant soldier who, with his wealthy wife, built a jewel-like statement-palace in Torrijos, near Toledo, right at the very geographic heart of Spain. It was a palace that spoke to the confidence of the nation and its heritage, a nation proud of its Islamic and Christian histories, proud of the cosmopolitan complexity of its outlook. In the palace's key salons, Cárdenas installed opulent ceilings of carved Iberian pine, created from hundreds of painted geometric elements, that spoke to that glorious history.

As we have seen already, one of these ceilings is now installed at V&A Storehouse (fig. 36). It is as sumptuous and high-status as the great religious ceilings that were being painted in central Italy in the same period, and which celebrated similarly grand ideas. The Torrijos ceiling is a flamboyant geometric map that plays with symmetry and pattern development, evocative of the mathematical innovations that were redefining the age. Finished in gilt and paint, designed to carry your eyes upward, it is as audaciously close to perfection as the human hand would allow. It echoes the Muslim cultures in which mathematics was a major creative arena, in which depictions of the human body were not the norm; this is a conceptual map of the world and our relationship to it, mathematical cosmology against which we can measure ourselves. Although its owners and commissioners were prominent Catholics, it is a delicate, interwoven tapestry of Islamic and Christian motifs. It is a statement that does not seek to diminish the culture of its commissioners' past, or their adversaries, but confidently acknowledges their complex heritage. It represents a kind of creative confidence that balances its opulence with humility – a different kind of self-belief that is grounded in a worldly sensitivity. It is a gloriously confident statement by a globally invested couple at the very epicentre of a globally invested state that embraces a complex heritage and projects a future fuelled by big ideas.

The Torrijos ceiling carries its complex body of influences with ease and confidence. Where there might have been the possibility of tension in the accommodating of these strong narratives, there is self-belief. For a community dealing with dramatic change, this is the perfect response: a space of reflection and catharsis that is inspired by the region's cosmopolitan, expansive history.

In 2023, the architect and writer Shahed Saleem, the designer of several mosques across London, set out to mine the V&A collections and archives for objects that might speak to one of his great sources of inspiration: historic Islamic architecture. He has created mosques in a broad range of contexts, from re-purposing a variety of older buildings to finding the appropriate architectural response to new spaces. And although he has designed for a variety of contexts, he has always sought to turn his buildings into the sort of environments that people seek out and then want to return to. It has left him with an interest, and an expertise, in the histories of mosques and why they are loved. As Saleem explains, 'I have tried to incorporate references to traditional and recognizable Islamic art and architecture, but to combine it with contemporary materials and style. By doing this I am trying to design buildings that can be understood in diverse ways, and that are multivocal; they speak numerous languages.'[26]

There have been mosques in Britain since the late nineteenth century, and their number has grown with a steady flow of Muslim immigrants. Today, this British community is some 4 million strong, and its members practise across the country in more than 1,800 mosques. 'The more I looked at mosques across the country,' Saleem continues, 'the more I saw buildings that defied all notions of convention and taste, usually self-designed and built by highly marginalised and economically deprived communities. In this I saw great resilience, determination and inventiveness. These communities were creating new architectural meanings by drawing from their own lived experience and according to their own rules.'[27]

Saleem began an excavation of the V&A collections in order to recover forgotten histories, a process that was also an exercise in the recovery of cultural confidence. He resolved to create a mosque pavilion to host Ramadan celebrations at the V&A, to create a structure that faced into the vast body of Islamic objects and Islamic reference material within the museum. A priority for Saleem was 'recognising the histories and perspectives of those who have been traditionally marginalised ... Decolonisation ultimately is about giving up power and giving back, returning territory and compensating for losses inflicted on the colonised. Architecture's role in this process must also be recognised and articulated as part of the decolonisation process.'[28] A mechanism for that was the V&A collections.

The collections inspired Saleem to design a building that dealt with these marginalized histories while also feeling truly new (fig. 37). The component parts of his mosque are recreated, reimagined fragments from across the Muslim world. Together, however, they form a vivid and arresting single structure that acknowledges the complexity of Islam and, with that, the wide array of journeys taken by those Muslim families who have made their homes in the United Kingdom. As Saleem notes, 'The Ramadan Pavilion is a representation of the dynamic history of the mosque in Britain, through adaptations and ad hoc conversions to new buildings.'[29] Saleem sought to reconstitute these pieces into a confident, complex, cathartic whole. It is a new structure but fashioned from old elements. The perfect analogue of a religion that is constantly being remade.

Objects and their stories are powerful. Kente, a traditionally brightly coloured, hand-woven cloth from West Africa, has become synonymous with regional confidence. It has grown over recent generations to be adopted

37.

SHAHED SALEEM (b. 1971)

TOP: Sketchbook: pencil, pen, felt tip, watercolour, 12.5 × 20.7 cm (binding)
BOTTOM: The Ramadan Pavilion at the V&A, 2023

by many people of African descent across the diaspora as a spiritual symbol of racial pride and confidence. This ensemble, comprised of an Ewe Kente-inspired coat and a red cotton blouse and trousers, comes from Imane Ayissi's Spring/Summer 2017 collection entitled 'Asseulenn', meaning 'crossing' (fig. 39). Ayissi wanted to use the collection to create a dialogue between African, Asian and European cultures, playing with common motifs such as squares. For the collection, Ayissi brought together many different materials, from vintage kimono fabrics from Japan to kitas from the Ivory Coast and Kente cloth from Ghana, all sourced from collectors. Known for his glamorous collections that mix beautiful indigenous African textiles with classic French couture techniques and silhouettes, Ayissi has said of his work that 'fashion would be my way to tell African stories and show another version of African cultures.'[30] Another ensemble, this time from Ayissi's Autumn/Winter 2019 collection, 'Mbeuk Idourrou', explores the role of volume in creating presence, taking as its inspiration the Senegalese grand boubou and Japanese kimono (fig. 38). The palazzo trousers and cape are fuchsia satin, and the cape and top are fringed with dyed pink raffia from Madagascar. The bold colour and large volume of the cape speak to the theme of the collection: 'Mbeuk Idourrou' can be translated as 'he or she who wears a garment that is impressive', a saying that references the idea that clothes reflect not only the social status of the wearer, but also the success of their community.

Mussolini hoped that the obelisk of Axum would tell a story about his nation's might, its confidence. But it became a symbol of shame, a symbol of Fascism. After Mussolini's death at the end of the Second World War, the United Nations brokered a deal for the return of the stele. It took until the early twenty-first century for it to be dismantled, returned and reinstalled in Axum. Today, it serves as a different kind of marker: it looks back at the great history of Ethiopia, but it also serves to acknowledge the indefatigability and quiet confidence of the Ethiopian people in the face of such an oppressive force. It is a monument to loss, to hubris and to learning from history.

And that wisdom of learning, of building confidence in complex circumstances, is something that has driven Shahed Saleem. He has sought to build back a lost and fragmented narrative. The spaces he has constructed also echo some of the confident values reflected in the Torrijos ceiling; they are creative declarations that announce a sense of standing in the world. They accommodate seismic change, but are also symbols that bolster self-worth, pride and confidence in the face of great cultural complexity. They are about both our fluid, shifting identities and our changing politics that, in turn, are set against things that simply do not change: the value of global inclusive thinking, the powerful hybrid creativity that is an outcome of such thinking, and the timeless importance of listening out for the quieter voices.

38 & 39.

IMANE AYISSI (b. 1969)

OPPOSITE: Ensemble from ‘Mbeuk Idourrou’ collection, 2019.
Pink silk, linen and raffia cape and trousers

ABOVE: Ensemble from ‘Asseulenn’ collection, 2017.
Kente coat, cotton top and trousers

ALESSANDRO MICHELE (b. 1972) IN COLLABORATION WITH TREVOR ANDREW (TROUBLE ANDREW) (b. 1979)

Gucci tote bag, 2016. Leather, 45 × 42.5 × 16 cm

The former Olympic snowboarder and street artist Trevor Andrew (Trouble Andrew) is also known as GucciGhost, an alter ego inspired by the artist's passion for the Gucci fashion brand. Alessandro Michele, former creative director of Gucci, instigated a collaboration with Andrew after seeing his interpretation of the Gucci branding painted on bags, clothes and street objects. In concert with Michele, Andrew applied his version of the double 'G' Gucci logo, the phrase 'Life is Gucci' and the word 'REAL' onto Gucci bags and outfits for the brand's Autumn/Winter 2016 runway collection, reflecting his confidence and belief in the GucciGhost project and its reality on the catwalk.

REAL
GUCCI

OFF-WHITE C/O VIRGIL ABLOH™

VIRGIL ABLOH (1980–2021)

'Puffy Fanny Pack' by Off-White, 2019.
Nylon belt bag, 16 × 30 × 7 cm

Street-style brand Off-White, founded by Virgil Abloh in 2013, is known for creating luxury streetwear, transforming wearable and familiar items such as rucksacks, backpacks and bum bags, as well as T-shirts and tracksuits, into sought-after fashion statements. Intentionally straddling worlds and definitions, the name 'Off-White' reflects Abloh's confident remixing of styles and influences, streetwear and haute couture, adeptly sampling from different cultural mores to create a revolutionary fashion language.

Breath

The first and last thing that humans struggle to do, so deeply fundamental to human life that we take it for granted, drawing breath is the inspiration for a wide array of creative output. Here we examine its place in literature, art and design as a recurrent metaphor for life itself.

One of the most memorable, if minor, characters of nineteenth-century fiction is Pip, the African American cabin-boy onboard the whaling ship *Pequod* in Herman Melville's epic novel, *Moby Dick*. We do not know if a particular person inspired the character, but young sailors like Pip would not have been unusual at the time. There were as many as 3,000 African Americans serving on the hundreds of ships that worked the rich fishing grounds of the North Atlantic – about a third of the fishing workforce. Pip is not the focus of the book, yet he sets the early emotional temperature of the novel: we share his fear, his awe and his wonder at the world.

Although he is one of the *Pequod*'s least experienced crew members, Pip is ordered to step in for an injured colleague on a whale hunt. Told to find his place in a tiny scouting boat, he is understandably terrified. You feel his fear on the page. And there were certainly things to be concerned about. This was a tiny vessel, propelled by the blades of oars up vast vertical waves in pursuit of whales before dropping down into the bellies of ferocious, frothing cauldrons of churning water, over and over again. In the heat of the hunt, in a blind panic, Pip leaps from the boat into the water, only to find his limbs hopelessly tangled in the harpoon line. Amid the chaos, the crew are forced to cut the line to save his life, only to lose the whale.

Later, Stubbs, the second mate, pulls Pip aside for a quiet word: 'We can't afford to lose whales by the likes of you; a whale would sell for thirty times what you would,

Pip, in Alabama.'[31] But a few days later, still traumatized by what happened, Pip jumps into the sea once more. This time he does not jump in panic:

> The sea had jeeringly kept his finite body up, but drowned the infinite of his soul. Not drowned entirely, though. Rather carried down alive to wondrous depths, where strange shapes of the unwarped primal world glided to and fro before his passive eyes ... and among the joyous, heartless, ever-juvenile eternities, Pip saw the multitudinous, God-omnipresent ... He saw God's foot upon the treadle of the loom, and spoke it.[32]

Pip is again plucked from the sea, rescued, but is never the same. Although the majority of his shipmates subsequently pass the episode off as the delusional rantings of a child, Melville leaves the reader with the suspicion that in the depths, beyond the point where his lungs gave out and the last bubble of air left his lips, Pip had indeed encountered something important, something supernatural – a consciousness that understood what it was to be breathless, hunted – and had returned a changed person. He had returned as a living ghost; a being, both blessed and damned.

Pip represents one of the many millions of young people of African descent whose lives, freedom or heritage were taken by the Atlantic. A decade before Melville wrote *Moby Dick*, the artist J. M. W. Turner had memorialized the throwing overboard of 130 enslaved Africans in the painting *Slave Ship (Slavers Throwing Overboard the Dead and Dying, Typhoon Coming On)* (1840; Museum of Fine Arts, Boston) because they were worth more in insurance than as living beings (fig. 40). The drawing of breath is the first and last thing we ever do; it is fundamental to life. Yet throughout history, it has been an act that some have felt they possessed the right to take, and which others have had to fight for.

On 17 July 2014, a group of New York Police Department officers approached Eric Garner, a 43-year-old African American who was standing on a Staten Island street corner. This in itself was not remarkable; over recent years, he had been arrested more than thirty times for a range of minor offences. The officers later claimed that, on that particular Thursday, they had suspicions that Garner was illegally selling individual cigarettes. The situation escalated very quickly, and one of the police officers, Daniel Pantaleo, grabbed Garner by the neck, pulling him to the ground and placing him in a choke-hold. The last words that Eric Garner managed to say before his death were, 'I can't breathe.' He would repeat them a further ten times. By the end of the decade, the same final words had been uttered by three more individuals: Javier Ambler, on 28 March 2019; Elijah McClain, on 24 August 2019; and Manuel Ellis, on 3 March 2020. Each of these individuals was an African American man who had been stopped randomly by a police officer on a US city street.

40.

J.M.W TURNER (1775–1851)

Slave Ship (Slavers Throwing Overboard the Dead and Dying, Typhoon Coming On), 1840.
Oil on canvas, 90.8 × 122.6 cm

On 25 May 2020, George Floyd, a 46-year-old African American musician, was stopped by Derek Chauvin, a white police officer, and three of his colleagues from the Minneapolis Police Force. The choreography of the situation was well rehearsed; this had happened on so many other streets across America, over many, many decades. The situation unravelled at speed. Within moments, Chauvin had wrestled Floyd to the ground, placed his knee on Floyd's neck and applied his body-weight. The strangely relaxed demeanour of the officer, as he looked around without moving his knee, would send chills around the world when the footage was released. Floyd did not struggle, he offered no resistance, he was utterly compliant. Eventually, he stopped asking to stand up; eventually, he stopped pleading for breath; eventually, he stopped calling for his mother. But the knee across his neck did not move, cutting the oxygen to his lungs and then his brain. Although this situation was all too familiar, what happened next was not expected. In the middle of a global pandemic, a contagion that arbitrarily took the breath from millions, this conscious, clinical suffocation, played out in slow motion and delivered on our behalf, seemed utterly unacceptable. The death of George Floyd triggered the largest racial justice protests in the United States since the Civil Rights Movement, followed by marches, protests and events that rippled out across the world. Many nations were able to sympathize: they could identify their own George

Floyds, their own anger, shame and frustration. There were statements from heads of state, there were speeches in parliaments, companies published commitments. In the words of Floyd's daughter, Gianna, spoken during a meeting with President Biden, 'Daddy changed the world.' And she was right: this century is only a quarter of the way through its passage, and yet one of its truly iconic images has already made its mark.

Fred Hoffman, in his writings about Jean-Michel Basquiat, reflected that the American artist showed an 'innate capacity to function as something like an oracle distilling his perceptions of the outside world down to their essence and, in turn, projecting them outward through his creative acts'.[33] Sometimes, as with Turner's *Slave Ship*, artists capture an ambient mood, an anxiety, and do so in ways that offer welcome coherence to a widely held sentiment. At other times, as Hoffman implies, they can do something even more extraordinary: they can articulate a societal concern before it becomes widespread. In 2014, some six years before George Floyd's murder, Greg Bunbury, an East London graphic designer, created a poster featuring the last words of Eric Garner, 'I can't breathe', repeated eleven times (with a haunting, incomplete final instance) (fig. 41). Each iteration is capitalized and set on a separate line with no exclamation mark – white text on blood-clot red. It is chilling. Garner's words are final, complete statements that need to be heard, to be listened to. Although the poster was created in 2014, it wouldn't

41.

GREG BUNBURY (b. 1976)

I Can't Breathe, 2014; printed 2023.
Poster, C-type print, 71 × 50 cm

be until 2020, amid the outrage that followed the murder of George Floyd, that it truly, globally resonated. It was an image that captured the deep, guttural, worldwide exhalation of anger at the racism we seemed to have grown accustomed to, so much so that many could not see it. It took the lives of several young men, the brilliance of Greg Bunbury and the presence of the Black Lives Matter movement to shift the dial. And like Turner's painting, Bunbury's work is about recording: without the painting, without the mobile phone video, without the poster, these things would in large part go unnoticed. The artist's role in creating spaces for us to take stock, to breathe, to reimagine and remember, is important.

At the time that Bunbury was creating his iconic image, Esther Rolinson had begun a different but conceptually connected exploration of breath. Her interest lay less in division within societies and more in interconnectedness. Rolinson's *Breathing the breath of others* is a 21 × 28-cm map, a digitally manipulated pencil drawing of the passage of shared breaths (fig. 42). Although the map does not depict people, it captures their presence through the gaseous trail that the pattern of their inhalation and exhalation of air leaves behind; we see the spread of the contents of lungs through the atmosphere, to be inhaled by others, over and over again. As Bunbury had foreseen the 2020 George Floyd moment, Rolinson also seems to have intuited the anxieties connected to the sharing of breath that would accompany the Covid-19 pandemic.

Her image seems to capture that pandemic neurosis: on the one hand a fear of others, and on the other a simultaneous interconnectedness.

When Pip jumped overboard and descended into Melville's marginal world, he was not seeking death but an alternative destiny. He wanted to discover a space that was safe, that might isolate him from the harshness of the world. And perhaps when George Floyd called out for his mother, it was a similar plea for an alternative destiny. It is this relationship to breathing that designer Emma Woffenden captures in *Breath*, a work that explores separation (fig. 43). For this astounding glass sculpture, Woffenden constructed a bell jar designed to separate, control and contain an atmosphere but remain transparent. It is an affecting visual essay in human isolation and connectedness. It echoes the process of breathing, the idea of the body being a vulnerable vessel for life, but it also speaks affectingly to the tensions in our society. We need and depend on one another, and yet we seek to build and maintain hierarchies and barriers to contain and exclude. When Derek Chauvin knelt on George Floyd's neck and denied him breath, he did so on our behalf. He believed that he was doing his duty. He believed that we would agree that certain individuals were inherently both a threat and somehow lesser: that they could be abused, enslaved and thrown to their deaths from the decks of ships; that they could be stopped without cause; and that he had the right to extinguish the breath in their lungs. And yet,

42.
ESTHER ROLINSON (b. 1971)
Breathing the breath of others, 2014; printed 2016.
Digitally manipulated pencil drawing, 28 × 21.8 cm

43.

EMMA WOFFENDEN (b. 1962)

Breath, c. 1994–95. Glass, 25.5 × 19 cm (diameter at base) although he sought Floyd's silence, his supplication, his utter compliance, Floyd's final whisper, 'I can't breathe', would echo out around the world, to be repeated as a defiant statement by millions, become an iconic image, to infect the psyche and be adopted as a slogan and manifesto for a generation. And perhaps the most powerful manifestation of this phenomenon was the spread of raw footage of Floyd's murder, and an incredible poster that was like a visual exhalation of air, a scream of anger, a roar of defiance, an aching visceral howl at all the loss and lessons missed over the centuries.

DESIGNED BY ZHIJUN WANG (b. 1982)

Single-edition face mask constructed out of materials from a CLOT x Nike Air Force 1 PRM (premium) sneaker, 2020. Silk, leather and metal, 13.5 × 20 cm

Zhijun Wang started making sneaker masks in 2013 to increase awareness about the level of air pollution in Beijing. Having begun his career designing customized sneakers, Wang noticed that the lightweight, durable and breathable fabric used for the upper part of sneakers would be an ideal fabric for face masks.

During the Covid-19 pandemic, Wang's sneaker masks took on a new significance as design interventions. In April 2020, Wang and his wife, Yutong Duan, began an open-access project called 'Maskology – Everyone Can Make a Mask', providing a mask template in eight different languages on their website. The website received more than 25,000 views and downloads, with people from across the world sharing their 'Maskology' masks on Instagram.

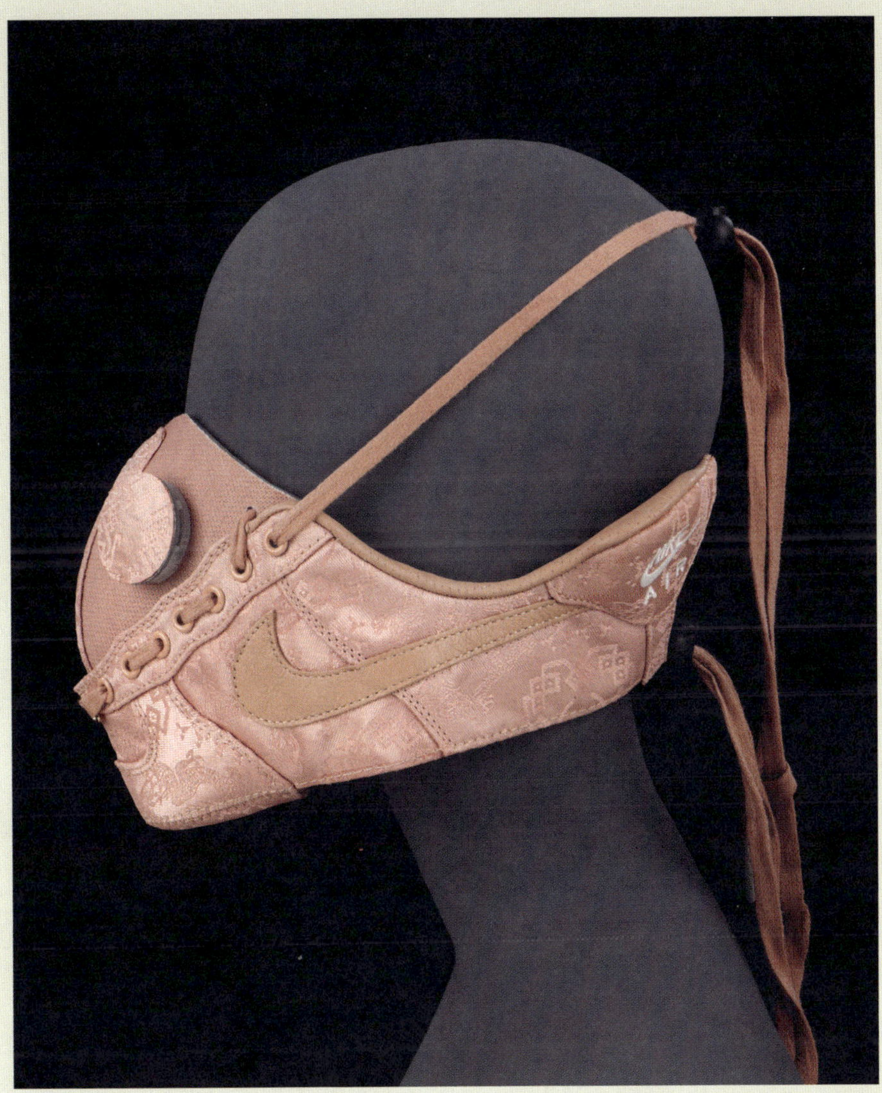

KEEP AMERICA BEAUTIFUL
STOP AIR POLLUTION
LOVE
KEEP OUR CITY CLEAN
COUGH COUGH

'POLLUTION' FURNISHING FABRIC
MADE BY AVONDALE MILLS INC., 1971

Roller-printed cotton

In April 1970, some 22 million people took to the streets of America to protest against the environmental destruction they were witnessing. The first Earth Day is often heralded as the beginning of a modern environmental movement, formed in the wake of the civil rights, women's rights and anti-war movements in the United States. This furnishing fabric from 1971, produced by North American textile manufacturers Avondale Mills Inc., features an urban scene of skyscrapers and smoke, overflowing dustbins, road sweepers and street graffiti demanding 'KEEP OUR CITY CLEAN'. Two protestors hold placards reading 'STOP AIR POLLUTION' and 'KEEP AMERICA BEAUTIFUL', one wearing a gas mask. In contrast, a man and a woman embrace beside a stream, surrounded by flowering foliage.

Respect

Sustaining a creative practice can be vital to supporting a sense of self in the face of restriction or oppression. This is the story of artist Ibrahim El-Salahi and his experience as a political prisoner, and of Kenny Zulu Whitmore, who has spent more than forty-five years in the Louisiana State Penitentiary for a murder that he claims he did not commit. In this chapter, we interrogate how we choose to reflect worth, how we demonstrate value to others, and how creativity in an environment that means to confine and diminish can offer freedom via a demand for acknowledgment and respect.

While serving as under-secretary for culture in the government of Sudan, Ibrahim El-Salahi was imprisoned without trial. El-Salahi was always first and foremost an artist, a painter. But as one of the most successful contemporary Sudanese artists working in a relatively fragile and volatile environment, he sought to use his reputation and position to advocate for the culture sector. It would prove to be a mistake. Wrongly accused of involvement in an anti-government coup by the Communist Party in 1975, he was stripped of his political role and confined to a cell in the notorious Kober Prison, one of oldest and the toughest jails in Sudan. In the months after the failed *coup d'état*, when the atmosphere was febrile and the government was looking to demonstrate its reach and ruthlessness, El-Salahi was simply in the wrong place at the wrong time.

Kober Prison was the dark, dark hole where supposed enemies of state were systematically thrown by the powers that be, some never to re-emerge. Originally a colonial jail, it had a regime that was designed to break its inmates, bit by agonizing bit. Its former residents have included many senior ministers and civil servants. El-Salahi, who had championed Sudanese visual culture through his art and his actions, was confined to a cell for an indefinite period and told that he could not write, draw or paint; he was also informed that the punishment for non-compliance would be severe. But as weeks turned to months, as the harshness of the regime began to take

44.

IBRAHIM EL-SALAHI

Prison Notebook, 1976. Notebook with thirty-eight ink-on-paper drawings, 28.7 × 17 cm (each page, approx.), 28.7 × 18.1 × 2.9 cm (overall, closed) its toll on his mind and body, El-Salahi began to hanker after creative opportunities. He longed to draw and paint once more. One day, while in the prison exercise yard, he found a pen. This began a clandestine campaign of gathering up his guards' discarded cigarette papers and secreting them in his pockets, up his sleeves, within his closed fists, whenever he could. Pen and paper were all he needed to forge a kind of freedom, to regain his dignity amid the daily horrors. He started to draw secretly while alone in his cell (fig. 44). He understood the risk, he knew that the cost of getting caught might be his life, but during his time in prison he had come to discover that, for him, life and art were synonymous. To maintain his psychological equilibrium and sense of self, he needed to make, and to continue to make, art. It was art as an expression of agony, as an act of defiance, as a way of making a record – and, perhaps most importantly, as a means of preserving self-respect. We don't just need art in our lives, we also need to create it.

Within months of El-Salahi entering Kober Prison in 1975, Kenny Zulu Whitmore, a young African American, was beginning a life sentence in an equally notorious jail, the Louisiana State Penitentiary. Angola, or 'the Last Slave Plantation' as the penitentiary was also known by its inmates, was (and remains) one of the toughest, most brutal prisons in the United States. And for Whitmore, as a young man beginning a sentence with a recommended term of 225 years, it must have been terrifying. But fifty years later, despite protesting his innocence, despite multiple appeals for a retrial, for parole, for clemency, Whitmore remains in prison, having spent almost forty of those years confined to a 9 × 6-foot cell. At its most extreme, the prison regime would allow him just occasional exercise, and even that was conducted in such a way as to remind the inmates of their incarceration. As Whitmore has lamented, '[I exercise] three times a week. You can only wear a T-shirt and shorts under the orange jumpsuit. You are fully restrained – waist chain, and leg irons. Only the leg irons are removed.' When asked how he holds onto his sanity, spending much of his life confined alone to a cell, he replied, 'I use my pen.'[34] Like El-Salahi, he has turned to art. Some decades ago, Whitmore began to make small stainless-steel dog tags (fig. 45). Each is decorated with the words 'Free Zulu' in relief, set into a textured background. They are simple but very affecting.

For Whitmore, his new-found skill was at first simply part of a campaign to bring attention to his plight with the hope of negotiating his freedom. Dog tags were first adopted during the American Civil War in the 1860s. They were traditionally worn in pairs around a soldier's neck. Stamped with the soldier's name, battalion and number, they were more than just name tags. If the worst happened and the soldier was killed in action, his fellow soldiers could take a single tag with them, leaving one on the body for identification. In this way, the soldier's

45.
KENNY ZULU WHITMORE (b. 1946)
'Free Zulu' pendant, 2014.
Stainless-steel pendant and chain

family could be told the news, and the body would stand the best possible chance of being recovered, reunited with loved ones and buried. Perhaps Whitmore does not want to be forgotten, and his single dog tags are a plea to be remembered, a plea for freedom, a hope that we might help to reconnect him with his lost life. But, like El-Salahi, his art is also about respect. In his early life, Whitmore was an activist – a man who sought to push back against the barriers and prejudices that he encountered as an African American. He sought respect: he wanted to be worthy of acknowledgment, dignity and care. Although they are a plea for freedom, one senses that after half a century in jail, Whitmore's dog tags are also an undimmed plea for acknowledgment. In extremis, when people's voices have been dimmed by challenging circumstances, many have sought to broker respect from others and to maintain self-respect through making. And the subtle but deliberate beauty of these dog tags would seem to be Whitmore markedly asserting a right to dignity.

Art is perhaps the most beautiful and palpable instantiation of our primal existential drive. When we need it, art can be gloriously freeing; it can be a potent source of pride, of catharsis and self-realization. Perhaps that is why, throughout history, jails, asylums, detention centres and workhouses have fostered, against all odds, rich traditions of creative practice among their inmates. Over the course of the nineteenth century, when prison culture in the industrialized world took shape, art played a significant role within the prison regime. The English painter Richard Dadd, who spent extended periods detained in Bethlem and Broadmoor psychiatric hospitals (being treated for what was likely schizophrenia), created some of the most powerfully escapist fantasy landscapes of the Victorian era, behind bars. In the early 1800s, the Quaker and social reformer Elizabeth Fry instigated wide-reaching campaigns to promote needlework as a useful skill for incarcerated women. Carpentry, joinery and furniture-making were encouraged in French prisons during the latter years of the nineteenth century. In the most illiberal and conservative of centuries, the window of self-improvement and self-respect, through creativity, was afforded its condemned. Fry was adamant that 'Some remuneration for their work, even during their continuance in confinement, will be found to act as a powerful stimulus to a powerful and persevering industry.'[35]

Exposure to these kinds of creative opportunity would have a profound impact on prisoners. When one of the many female felons that Fry had trained in needlework was being transported to Australia, she wrote of how she used the time to craft a patchwork quilt. These quilts would often be group endeavours, and some, like the Rajah Quilt, crafted by twenty-nine women on board the convict ship the *Rajah*, were of astounding quality (fig. 46). It is a painstakingly engineered and deeply complex work that shows the kind of care and love that the Victorian penal system was simply not known for.

46.

THE RAJAH QUILT (DETAIL), 1841

Cotton patchwork and appliquéd bed cover or coverlet, 325 × 337.2 cm

47.

HMP WANDSWORTH QUILT, 2010

Pieced, appliquéd and embroidered cotton and linen, 195 × 260 cm

In 2010, in collaboration with the charity Fine Cell Work, the V&A commissioned the HMP Wandsworth Quilt (fig. 47). A collective response to the relationship between confinement and creativity, it speaks to the long tradition of prisoners collaborating on the creation of narrative quilts. Designed and made by inmates, the quilt was conceived to reveal something of the nature of incarceration, the importance of creative work and the possibilities of mutual respect. Speaking at the time of its creation, one of the contributing prisoners commented: 'The finished product will be the work of many hands. We are working together, showing each other colours, commenting on each other's work. It gives you a purpose to relate to other people. It's difficult talking to strangers but if you can do it with a reason it helps. You can learn from other people and teach them something as well. You feel you've advanced your knowledge and experience.'[36]

Each of these examples of creativity is a work that was defiantly made – art that was created as a way of reminding the world of the maker's plight. In part, they are affecting because of the autobiographical nature of their narratives, but also because they are stark reminders of how art is integral to both maintaining self-respect and brokering the respect of others.

There are of course many works of art that ascribe respect to someone other than the maker. So often in history, these have been powerful subjects who were lauded by society. Occasionally, however, an artist has deliberately chosen someone like you or me. In 2020, Kehinde Wiley, the Nigerian American portrait artist, began a project in East London. Two years earlier, Wiley had unveiled his portrait of President Obama, which would sit in the National Portrait Gallery in Washington DC alongside some of the most iconic American portraiture ever created. In East London, Wiley was looking for a different kind of subject. He has often sought out his subjects on city streets, selecting them from among the crowds. He chose Melissa Thompson after seeing her on a street in Dalston. Perceiving her to be someone who possessed a natural charisma and gravitas, Wiley painted her sitting on a throne-like armchair against a William Morris wallpaper (fig. 48). It is an image that subverts traditional portrait conventions in its choice of subject, and yet it sits comfortably as an image within the history of portraiture. Thompson looks at the viewer with a confidence of another age of portrait painting. Yet the yellow leaves of the wallpaper refuse to remain in the background, pushing their way into the foreground to embrace or even overcome her.

Kenny Zulu Whitmore was driven to his activism out of rage. He believed that people of African descent were not afforded the respect they deserved. And it is hard to argue with that. His act of making his dog tags is one of defiance, a refusal to lay down and be forgotten. Kehinde Wiley expresses some of that same anger on Melissa Thompson's behalf. She should not be forgotten, ignored,

48.

KEHINDE WILEY (b. 1977)

Portrait of Melissa Thompson,
from the series *The Yellow Wallpaper*, 2020.
Oil on linen, 265.5 × 201.8 cm

passed by in the street. She is a queen; she is noble on her own terms, deserving of the time of a great portrait artist, deserving of our time, our gaze, deserving of our, and society's, respect. She herself is not angry; she is somehow beyond that. Her natural nobility (perhaps the innate quality that Wiley saw on that London street) affords her a quiet inner peace, a kind of resolved self-respect. And yet those yellow leaves that seek to embrace her tie her to the same past, the same pressures and prejudices as so many other peoples of colour. But like Wiley's portrait of Obama, she possesses, deep within, something defiantly proud, confident and true; an innate understanding of the past, the pressures of the present, but an unyielding hope for the future.

And hope is important. Ibrahim El-Salahi would be released after serving six months in Kober Prison. There was no trial before, or at any time during, his incarceration. The visual essays he had begun to sketch on cigarette papers would not survive, but the memories of his incarceration became the basis of a complex and beautiful body of work that would define his art for a generation. That search for respect became a search on behalf of Sudan, for African humankind. His work connects his personal battle for respect with that of a nation. El-Salahi's canvases are cathartic essays on race, dignity, history and hope, which have been collected by some of the most significant galleries in the world. His personal journey into hell transcended the particularity of his plight to become a narrative with the power to touch us all. We arrive in the world alone, and will ultimately depart that way, and the profound isolation that we can encounter is one of the defining qualities of human existence. But some inspirational individuals never cease reaching out, trying to make connections. Both Whitmore and El-Salahi have faced long periods of isolation, but they found a way, through their art, to reach out beyond the confines of their cells and touch us, to make a beautiful record for posterity. And the core message they sought to convey was one of respect – both the self-respect they found through creativity, and the plea for universal respect for all people that is the core theme of their work.

FREE
RUHUL

My series Chalo Dilli is an exploration of the culture of dissent and protest in India. Since 2016, I have been interviewing and photographing Indians who come from across the country to protest at Jantar Mantar. (Harsha Vadlamani)

#FREEPALESTINE
#INDIASTANDSWITHPALESTINE

WHERE IS KAJOL?
"Bangladesh authorities should urgently locate the journalist Shafiqul Islam Kajol, who has been missing since March 10, 2020" (Human Rights Watch, 13.03.20)

BLACK
TRANS

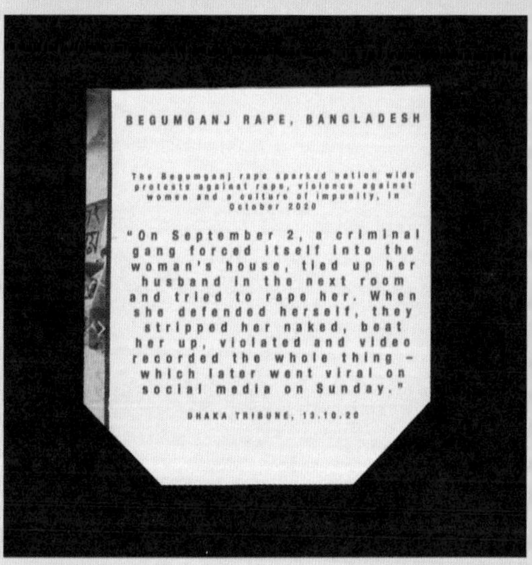
BEGUMGANJ RAPE, BANGLADESH
The Begumganj rape sparked nation wide protests against rape, violence against women and a culture of impunity, in October 2020
"On September 2, a criminal gang forced itself into the woman's house, tied up her husband in the next room and tried to rape her. When she defended herself, they stripped her naked, beat her up, violated and video recorded the whole thing – which later went viral on social media on Sunday."
DHAKA TRIBUNE, 13.10.20

SOFIA KARIM (b. 1976)

Samosa packets, part of the *Turbine Bagh* project, 2020–21. Printed paper, each 18 × 18 cm

Commonly made from scrap paper across South Asia, these samosa packets are printed with designs that include images, statements and poetry sent to Sofia Karim by campaigners, writers and artists from around the world. Inspired by a samosa packet she bought in Dhaka that was made of court listings, detailing cases between the state and its citizens, Karim began making her own packets to tell stories of resistance when her uncle, photographer Shahidul Alam, was imprisoned for his activism in Bangladesh.

Turbine Bagh was originally planned as a demonstration for the Turbine Hall at London's Tate Modern in solidarity with Shaheen Bagh, a grassroots, women-led Indian resistance movement against authoritarianism. It has since evolved into a platform for political art and activism, its scope expanding to address a range of interconnected stories and protest movements, including the Palestinian struggle against occupation, Black Lives Matter, the plight of Rohingya refugees, and individual cases of illegal imprisonment or censorship.

Family

Design holds us together. It is central to family ceremonies, links us through inherited traditions and identifies us as belonging to a particular group. Family links are made not just through blood but through ceremony, and what sets families apart from each other can be informal or codified. Modern interpretations of family can be very broad: as much as you cannot choose your genetic family, design can help us choose our own intimate social group.

49.

NATASHA KERR (b. 1986)

At the End of the Day, 2007. French linen hanging, transfer-printed, silkscreen-printed, hand-painted, hand-stitched, 75 × 110 cm

The word 'curator' is undoubtedly overused, but perhaps its overuse is understandable. It represents a range of drives, thought processes and compulsions that are primal, fundamental to humanity. We simply need (and love) to collect, collate, conserve and curate things. Collections make sense of us and those we care about. At the heart of most families are collections: informal bodies of loved things that are important to our shared stories. The artist Natasha Kerr has dedicated a significant amount of time to creating work that celebrates the need to hold onto our family stories through stored caches of objects (fig. 49). There are family albums, collections of crockery, drawers of old lace and embroidery; maybe you have inherited jewelry or passed down furniture? Or maybe you have your hidden treasure folded into a sock at the back of a drawer, alongside the engraved watch, or the broken carriage clock, by the scuffed box of wedding rings, all of which you will pass on to someone that you care about. Perhaps you are fortunate enough to have family heirlooms – the treasured boxes of old family documents, the wardrobes of grand dresses and smart suits. And, possibly forgotten, the foxed albums of sepia photographs, the frayed sheaf of textile that sat on a coffin in a wake a generation ago, or the faded tablecloth with the patches of vivid hues trapped beneath candle wax.

This collection of delicate objects belonged to the Nugée family, Huguenot tailors who emigrated from Bordeaux to Cork between 1748 and 1752 and made a name for themselves with 'Nugée's waistcoats' in the early nineteenth century (fig. 50). The objects were preserved following the wedding of Edith and Francis Nugée in August 1854 to become part of the family's history – every object loved and treasured, reflections of the family bond across generations. You don't need to be a clairvoyant or a social anthropologist to discern the nature and quality of rich object histories: we all recognize them; we all know, across generations, the importance of the material evidence that families leave behind. And in those special moments, when we are jolted back across the chapters of our family history, it is so often loved objects that catalyse those journeys.

There are similar traditions in many regions of the world. Family and making go hand in hand, but there is something about the way in which fabric can connect us across generations that is particularly special. In Europe and the United States, quilting has also traditionally been a social activity, creating objects that embody familial ties and relationships within a community. This mid-nineteenth-century American bridal quilt was made to celebrate the wedding of John Haldeman and Anna Reigart (fig. 51). It is decorated with what appear to be sunbursts, perhaps to suggest the dawning of a new chapter in the lives of the newly-weds. Quilts share with *bojagi* – traditional Korean wrapping cloths – the communal nature of their creative processes, as well as the reuse of otherwise disposable pieces of cloth. But they also share

50.

WEDDING ACCESSORIES FROM THE NUGÉE FAMILY, 1854

FROM TOP TO BOTTOM: wreath; wedding favours; shoes by Chapelle

51.

BED COVER (DETAIL), 1846–47

American cotton patchwork bride's quilt with appliqué, 255 × 265 cm the status of being humbly important, of being enhanced through handling, use and love. It is that beautiful, shared impulse that Mawuena Kattah, the British Ghanaian artist, celebrated in her ceramic tile piece *Aunty, Mum and Me Talking About My Fabric Collection* (fig. 52). Cloth holds a very important place in traditional West Africa households. It is the perfect vessel for carrying a community's shared imagination, its shared stories. Cloth would be used and worn on significant occasions and, over time, would come to be valued for that very reason. Even today, there are few other objects that have such intimate relationships with West African families – as the enduring material link between the many, and the most important, shared moments of their lives. Cloth might be the only material link between disparate events over decades, across generations. The most loved textiles offer a form of corroborative testimony that ties families across geography and time. You can see that celebrated in the work of the region's most successful artists, from El Anatsui and Yinka Shonibare to Ibrahim Mahama.

Here, however, Mawuena Kattah has used another, traditionally female West African creative medium, ceramics, to give us an intimate view of a group of Ghanaian women gathered around their cloth. She makes us aware that this group are not just friends, they are family – this is, as the work's title declares, 'Aunty, Mum and me talking'. You can imagine the conversation, the older aunt drawing beautiful stories from the fabric. In the right hands,

52.
MAWUENA KATTAH (b. 1975)
Aunty, Mum and Me Talking About My Fabric Collection, 2016.
Glazed ceramic tile frieze, 165 × 125 cm

every mark and tear can be read, mined, animated by the right aunty. West African cloth is the collected forensic evidence of a family's continuity, capturing everything in a single, beautiful thing: ancestry. Fabric can give focus and coherence to the lives of people united by blood, but separated by geography and death. And because both cloth and stories are portable, these West African ways of celebrating family can follow the migratory movements

53.
KENTE (DETAIL), *C.* 1950
Hand-woven cotton, 283 × 200 cm

54.
YINKA SHONIBARE (b. 1962)
Diary of a Victorian Dandy: 14.00 hours, 1998, printed 2012. C-type print, 122 × 183 cm

of the diaspora out across the world. In the very fragility of cloth is a reminder of the preciousness of African histories. Many first- and second-generation British Ghanaians will possess old pieces of Kente or Adire fabric that might have survived generations and many family relocations (fig. 53).

Yinka Shonibare has chosen to turn Mawuena Kattah's picture of intimacy and love of family inside out. He has examined what it is like to feel alienated, to be excluded, to be an immigrant and to feel far away from home. Inspired by William Hogarth's series of paintings, such as *A Rake's Progress*, *Diary of a Victorian Dandy* tells the story of an African in Britain: confident, dapper, handsome – holding forth among the elite at the very height of Empire (fig. 54). This is someone who is far away from family; but rather than take up a marginalized position, a place at the edge of the frame, he seeks centre-stage with an almost arrogant authority. The women swoon, the men hold their breath admiringly, hanging on his every word. He holds in his hand a sheaf of papers – an agenda, a thesis, a plan. He commands the floor, about to break the silence, gazing out towards new horizons, undaunted by his platform. Art is a powerful medium for defining who we are and how we see ourselves, but also for defining the groups to which we feel affiliated. Shonibare stakes a claim to us, to our attention and respect in a confident, even imperial act. We can negotiate and create our own families.

Part of the cleverness of Shonibare's work is that it reminds us that great art, like Mawuena Kattah textiles, can make us feel included, part of things. It can make us feel safe. The reason our mantlepieces, our attics and our cellars are full of things that take up space but do not serve a practical purpose (and which we would hate to lose) is because they tell our stories and make us feel part of something. Art simply does that better than anything else. But, simultaneously, art can do the opposite; it can inadvertently, or deliberately, exclude, diminish and marginalize others. Shonibare, simply by being himself and taking a position and pose within a traditional composition, looking out at us in that imperious way, leaves us with something to think about. Who are the subjects of the art that we treasure? It is so easy to get used to being part of the accepted narrative – to identify with the protagonist, the creator, the audience – that we can fall into the trap of becoming blind to our fortune and privilege.

Just after the Second World War, Klaus Maertens, a German army doctor, created a new kind of boot. The uppers were soft, supple leather, but the real innovation was the air-cushioned sole. In 1959, the patent was acquired by a British manufacturer, and Dr. Martens were born. The boots are now available in a variety of styles, but it is the 1460 – named after the date of its release, 1 April 1960 – that became iconic and the choice of tradesmen who spent long days on their feet (fig. 55). The exaggerated 'neck' and number of eyelets on the boots made a

55.
DOC MARTENS BOOTS, *C.* 1982
Leather with a composition sole

feature of the laces, while the beautifully finished welting and the parallel incised lines along the soles created an instantly recognizable look. Although they were exquisitely styled, the boots were practical and lasted, which spoke to their integrity. And thanks to their 'AirWair' soles, they were also comfortable – unlike many items of fashion – becoming even more comfortable with use. When they were worn by groups of young people, in black or red, the boots took on the air of a military uniform; and yet they seemed to sit in diametric opposition to anything connected to the armed forces. Perhaps because of the association with toil, to working-class roots, Dr. Martens became popular with skinheads, mods and punks; the boots were practical, but they also suggested a rejection

56.
GAVIN WATSON (b. 1965)
Micklefield, 1981; printed 2011.
Gelatin silver print, 60.9 × 50.1 cm

of middle-class values. And like so much iconic fashion, the 1460 came to define a cultural family, representing certain values and excluding others. Dr. Martens would be worn, ironically and subversively, by groups from both the Left and the Right, by those deeply political and by those flamboyantly not (fig. 56). Today, they continue to hold particular cultural currency for many, providing a potent yet simultaneously understated 'look' that states that, beneath the polish, the wearer maintains an edge.

Culture is a powerful, social coagulant, and whether one is part of a family or a more extended, informal group, there is no more potent way of defining a sense of belonging, of building bonds and of excluding others. It can be our flag and our shield, the symbol that makes our heart leap, that evokes a deep connectivity to those we love and respect. It is a natural human drive to want to define our people, who and what we are, and by extension who we are not. Over millennia, objects have been effectively deployed as our flags and badges, the symbols of our belonging. They might be the anglicized Dr. Martens shoes, but they become more than just footwear; they are signifiers of a sociological outlook, a particular predisposition. We can codify inclusivity in traditions of making, like *bojagi*; in the intimacy of sharing creative processes; or through the shared objects, like Ghanaian cloth, that inspire and represent stories. But also, like Yinka Shonibare, we can use creativity to assert who we are not, project how we wish to be, and build the kind of community and connective social fabric that we desire. Objects combined with memory are powerful: they can inspire love and laughter, they can mark and then recall significant life events. They alone witness and represent the joy, the melancholy of age and the reckoning with mortality and loss. These beloved objects are imbued with romance and nostalgia and the battle against time, with the irrational shared love of family and things.

BASANT KAUR SANDHU
(NÉE JEUNI KAUR SIDHU) (1899–1984)

Bagh (detail), woman's wedding headcover, *c.* 1915–20.
Cotton embroidered in floss silk

The *phulkari* (flower work) embroidery style was traditionally used by women of the Punjab to decorate garments for themselves and their families. Patterns ranged from simple abstracted florals to the exactingly geometric. A *phulkari* embroidered shawl would qualify as a *bagh* (garden) shawl when nearly the entire cotton ground had been covered in silk stitches. This *bagh* was generously given to the V&A by the granddaughter of the embroiderer, Jeuni Kaur Sindhu of Malke village, who made it in preparation for her wedding in 1920.

CHRISTENING BLANKET (DETAIL), 1620–50

Embroidered silk edged with bobbin lace

This seventeenth-century Italian christening blanket is made of red silk trimmed with silver-gilt bobbin lace, the narrow ends having deep scallops in the Genoese style. Embroidered symmetrical motifs of tulips enclosing a basket of flowers can be seen in each corner, above which are two broad bands filled with fruit and flowers, including pansies and daffodils, as well as peacocks, parrots and other birds.

Families wrapped their swaddled babies in christening blankets, or bearing cloths, for ceremonial occasions. Such blankets displayed the wealth and status of their owners, and would be treated with great care and passed down through the generations. This blanket belonged to the Muti Papazzurri (formerly Savorelli) family, who used it at the christening of their first-born sons. There was a second, blue blanket for younger sons and, possibly, another for daughters.

Food

There are designs that speak to human commonality and nourishment. The spoon is a very simple form that we rely on as an object of service, and yet it has found a very special place in our lives. Although the simplest of tools in terms of shape and design, it stands as a testament to human ingenuity. This is the story of a utensil as an act of hospitality and care.

It may be one of the great apocryphal stories of art history, but it is also one that is worth repeating whenever the opportunity arises. It was 1936, the Depression was rumbling on, the Spanish Civil War had just begun, Edward VIII was considering abdication, Jesse Owens had just won four gold medals at the Berlin Olympics, and at a wine bar in Paris, Picasso was joined by the Surrealist artist Méret Oppenheim. Two great artists, two great friends, they – like everyone else – realized that the world as they understood it was disintegrating and that the political poles were being reset. It felt momentarily as though the patterns that underwrite history had been suspended. Picasso noticed that Oppenheim's bracelet was fur-lined and remarked that anything could be covered in fur, 'even this cup'. It felt like a comment on an unsettled and unsettling time in history, and it became the catalyst for the creation of one of the most iconic and sensual pieces of Surrealist art, Oppenheim's *Object* (fig. 57). It is an artwork that invites us to imagine drinking from a fur cup; it asks us to imagine wet fur on our lips. It plays provocatively with ideas of consumption and sex, of civility and carnality. In a period when the world felt like it was teetering on the very edge, it somehow spoke to the careless indulgence of the age.

Some twenty years later, as the end of the Second World War gave way to a new world order, Salvador Dalí, the spiritual leader of the Surrealist movement, would make a similar aesthetic statement, again evoking the

57.
MERET OPPENHEIM (1913–1985)
Object, 1936. Fur-covered cup, saucer and spoon

58.
SALVADOR DALÍ (1904–1989)
Ménagère (Cutlery Set), 1957.
Silver-gilt cutlery set: two forks, two knives and two enamelled spoons

connection between sex and consumption. If you were to strip back the spoon in Oppenheim's *Object*, would Dalí's gilded spoon lay beneath? *Ménagère* is a Surrealist cutlery set that teases with its sexual allusions, echoing Botticelli's use of natural forms as sexual metaphor (fig. 58). Taken together, *Object* and *Ménagère* operate as metaphorical bookends for the Surrealist movement; they also straddle the Second World War, the greatest conflagration the world has ever seen, when resources were so limited. This was Oppenheim and Dalí passing comment on an age in which it felt as though we had lost our moral compass, and in which the purity of consumption took on a vivid potency.

When, during one of the darkest chapters of world history, the Surrealists looked to food for inspiration, they sought from it something of its primal beauty, its truth. Although they enjoyed the absurd, they could read the zeitgeist; they could understand the emotional value of food. Where politics and economics had failed, perhaps older systems for addressing emotional needs could be of importance. After all, if you wanted tell the story of humanity through collections of objects, what would you choose? And if one of our aspirations was to touch, to affect others, how might you go about it? As the Surrealists suggest, among the most compelling bodies of material culture that we could deploy to tell the human story is the spectrum of things we have developed for the gathering, preparation and consumption of food. The accoutrements of food have a potent place in the human story. The spoon in particular is a very simple form, one that we rely on as an object of service, yet the variety in its shape and design is a testament to human ingenuity. And as Oppenheim and Dalí suggest, within its form is something primal, connective.

If culture at its best inspires empathy, then the intimate connections that we can build through food preparation and consumption are perhaps culture at its most compelling and powerful. The food, crockery and cutlery that has been pulled from the compacted ash and pumice at Pompeii can close the two-millennium gap between us and those who were about to sit down to eat breakfast on the morning of the Vesuvius eruption. To be able to see the freshly baked bread, the dried chestnuts, figs and prunes that were about to be entombed by a vast pyroclastic cloud is affecting. Time and geography are inadequate barriers to our connection with such a basic human need as eating. The feasts depicted on ancient Egyptian walls, the utensils excavated from Iron Age graves, the surviving archaeological evidence of the meals of our pre-human ancestors – all are powerfully compelling. They point not only to our primal relationship to food, but also to the common cultural understanding of the rituals, the sharing, the empathy and the art that food can inspire.

The beauty of ancient stone blades or fashioned arrow heads, knapped with great love and care, remains immediate and vital. We understand why our ancestors would go to such lengths to craft something of such intimacy and unnecessary sophistication. When beauty was not necessary, humanity would work to find it. This desire to make and collect considered and beautiful things is something that is hard-wired into our being; and when combined with the primal intimacy of sharing food, it becomes profoundly potent. As soon as we had found ways to produce food in large quantities, to create a surplus, it ceased to simply be about sustenance; it also became about social connections, beauty and love. Food and the culture that surrounds it hold a unique place in our lives; food has the power to be both formal and intimate simultaneously. And while a meal might last moments, the artefacts and material culture that support and surround food consumption are the things that we treasure, that archaeologists exhume with bodies in the most ancient burial sites, and which, even after millennia, can still transport us back to the importance of meals that we might have shared.

The spoon, as we have noted, is particularly special – the piece of cutlery that we are first weaned on as a child and the implement that our helpers might use to feed us in our dotage. No blade, no teeth, no prongs. This is the item of cutlery that could never double as a weapon; if anything, it is an indulgent implement that celebrates the act of consumption by making it a sensual thing. The particular intimacy that spoons can invoke is exemplified in this quietly spectacular Inuit bone spoon (fig. 59). It was made by an Iñupiat artist who lived in the north-west region of Alaska, one of the most inhospitable places on Earth. This is a place where the elements concertedly conspire against life, making sharing and cooperation critical to survival. And this spoon is a celebration of communality. It has been suggested that it might be carved from mammoth ivory, which would make the material at least four thousand years old. It was made in the first quarter of the nineteenth century, a wide, shallow spoon for scooping and holding blubber – one of the few sources of fat available at the time – with the heads of a human and a seal as handles. Its maker must have known the rareness of mammoth tusk and sought to honour that rareness by making something special. In form, and symbolically, it is a celebration of sharing, of togetherness, of love. The choice to adorn the object with a human and seal head speaks to the necessary symbiosis that is the basis of survival in an inhospitable landscape. The two heads, the coming together of the two significant animal presences in the landscape, captures the balance between two primary predators.

In contrast, this wooden spoon is almost impossibly ornate, overly engineered and considered, yet it is also an object to be used (fig. 60). It was made to evoke a sense of luxury and to suggest intimacy. Made in Iran in the nineteenth century from boxwood or pearwood, it was used to consume one of the most luxurious desserts of its time: sherbet. 'Sherbet', 'sharbah' and 'şerbet' all derive from the Arabic word *shariba* (شرب), which means to have drunk or quenched one's thirst. And in the hot landscapes of the Middle East, one can imagine how a culture might develop around slaking one's thirst. Sherbet was made from fruit juices that were mixed with herbs and reduced with sugar to form a syrup. When preserved, these fruit syrups of quince, apple, pear or peach could be transported over hundreds of miles, carrying fresh scents and flavours

59.

SPOON OR SCRAPER, 1800–1826

Possibly carved mammoth ivory, 3 × 11 × 7 cm

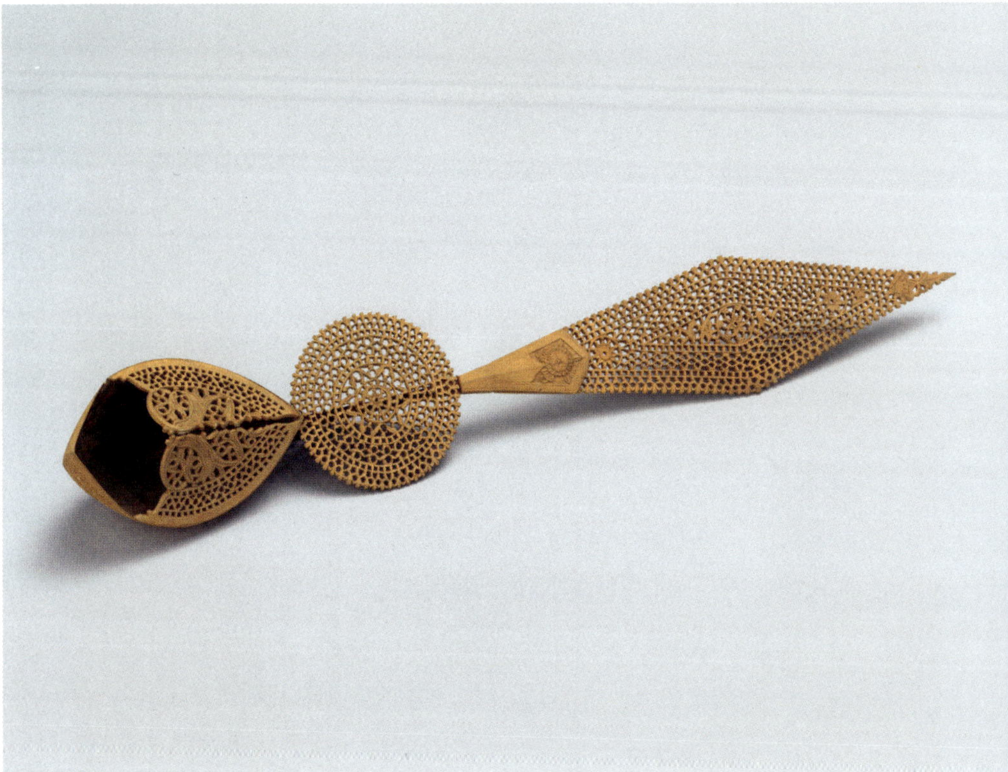

60.

SHERBERT SPOON, 1850–74

Carved pearwood, 36.5 × 8.5 cm

across the Middle East to be mixed with cold water or snow and then served. Sherbets are the forerunner of sorbets – refreshing, light and cool – and they would become popular across the Middle East, Europe and beyond.

This particular sherbet spoon is very finely carved, and it is likely that spoons of this quality were used by the elite and wealthy. They were placed in ceramic basins, their handles resting on the sides, their bowls immersed in the sherbet. Each guest would drink from a spoon and place it back in the basin. As much as being about the welcome consumption of a cool, sweet liquid, it was a way of spoiling one's guests. The luxurious ingredients, which could have travelled over long distances, the fine quality of the carving – all these things suggested the importance of the occasion and the guest. Here, as so often with food, it was in great part the presentation that was as important as what was being consumed. The first bite is with the eyes, but here we don't have to see the food. This spoon was made to make its users feel indulged, special, important, and it's hard not to believe that it would have worked.

It is perhaps understandable how such a generous utensil might acquire a special status in our lives, and in many cultures it has been given very significant ceremonial roles. At the 2023 coronation of King Charles III, for instance, in a tradition that dates back to the fourteenth century, a silver-gilt spoon was used to anoint the new monarch – part of a set of conventions conceived to evoke the investiture of King Solomon by Zadok the Priest. Although the spoon was rather humble, it was somehow symbolic of the cultural connective tissue between a biblical king and a living one. In India, this early seventeenth-century ceremonial spoon was crafted from gold with a resin core and inset with rubies, emeralds and diamonds along its edge (fig. 61). It was probably made in a Mughal court workshop in Northern India and might have been influenced by European ceremonial and coronation spoons.

Among the things that define humanity are abstract thinking, consciousness, social cooperation and tool use. These are the abilities, qualities and skills that give us learning and art. And it is in the humble spoon, in all its various forms, that those primal drives come together most potently. Food is fundamental to who and what we are, and perhaps the spoon is the most primal material manifestation of humanity. From the Inuit walrus-tusk carver, craving the sharing of blubber in Alaska, to the Mughal goldsmith providing ceremonial accoutrements, the spoon has spoken to us. Eating is one of the most oft-repeated things we do – and perhaps because of that, because of the rhythms and customs that surround the consumption of food, it has come to mean so much more than just nourishment.

61.
CEREMONIAL SPOON, *c.* 1600
18.6 cm (length)

PROBABLY PAINTED BY NICOLA DA URBINO
(ACTIVE 1520–37/38)

Trencher (opposite) and bowl (above), 1533–38.
Tin-glazed earthenware, 9.8 × 17.9 cm

As the production of maiolica flourished in Italy during the sixteenth century, ceramic wares such as this broth bowl and trencher (a flat plate used to cover a bowl) became an integral part of the rich and complex material culture associated with childbirth. As well as commemorating the birth of a child, the trencher and bowl would have been used to bring nourishing broth and other foods to a new mother. The trencher shows a childbirth scene, including a man casting a horoscope, while the inside of the bowl, which would have been slowly revealed to the mother as she ate, shows two nurses tending a newborn baby.

FRANCESCO DURANTINO (ACTIVE 16TH CENTURY)

Plate, 1540–45. Tin-glazed earthenware, 24.5 cm (diameter)

This plate, painted with scenes from the story of Psyche and Cupid, is representative of a shift in elite dining practices in sixteenth-century Italy. In contrast to an earlier custom of shared implements, dining services with individual plates, cutlery, napkins and place settings were introduced. As the diet of the wealthy members of society expanded, with new ingredients available from a widening global market, gastronomic literature became part of food culture, together with increasingly codified philosophical ideas on manners, cleanliness and hospitality. Maiolica dining services were often painted with antique narratives known as *istoriato* – ancient myths and histories that echoed the intellectual interests of the period and would likely be recognizable to diners.

Purpose

In all human groups, there are codes of behaviour that are understood to be a guide (or rulebook) for the best way of living. These codes have been transmitted through designs that are variously alluring, inspiring, moralizing, entertaining or terrifying. From the ubiquity of the Devil in medieval and early Renaissance European art to Hogarth's eighteenth-century prints, from a record of political turmoil to pioneering design practices, creativity is deployed to help us weigh up our choices, to reflect on and observe the world as it is, but also to inspire, restore and empower us to make it better.

62.
THOMAS J. PRICE (b. 1981)
A Place Beyond, 2023.
Bronze, 261.3 × 75.4 × 74.6 cm

From its conception, the V&A has always been more than a museum. It set out to be a platform for opportunity and transformation. Henry Cole, the museum's founder, engineered into its very fabric not just scholarship, collections and galleries, but also an aspiration to broker real change. He pioneered the introduction of cafés and open-access libraries, spaces where we might come to relax, be inspired, but also to find the tools to realize our aspirations. He wanted the V&A to be a toolbox of possibilities that could be used to change the world for the better. That gentle moral imperative has remained important to the institution, and at V&A East we have mined that spiritual DNA to inform our own founding purpose. When we looked to find a way of exemplifying Cole's beautiful, timeless vision, but to reimagine it for today, we sought out the artist Thomas J. Price. We wanted to commission a work that was not finger-wagging or strident, but a gentle, uplifting tribute to the rest of us. The result was a 5-metre-high version of Price's *A Place Beyond*, a bronze sculpture of a young woman (fig. 62). She looks like the kind of person who might pass unnoticed on a city street. She holds her phone in her hand; she gazes rightwards, towards the horizon, maybe to a place beyond. She is young – perhaps a symbol of hope, of the future – and in that gaze we see our own potential in hers.

Museums are not neutral spaces: their buildings, their collections and their curatorial narratives set out their priorities, their perspectives and the people they favour. You can see that manifest everywhere. The codes,

63.
STAINED-GLASS PANEL (DETAIL),
EARLY 15TH CENTURY
61.5 × 43.7 cm

ethics and mores that govern our lives can be reinforced or challenged by the curatorial and cultural choices we make. The most uplifting thing about the subject of *A Place Beyond* is that she seems devoid of negative karmic weight, unencumbered by societal concerns. She is no martyr or saint; she carries no burden on our behalf; we can see her lightness in her demeanour.

Lightness is important – it has a history. The ancient Egyptians adhered to the practice of the weighing of souls.

They would perform a ceremonial exercise on the bodies of the recently deceased, removing and placing the heart on a set of scales to be measured against the weight of a feather. The hope would be that, like the subject of Price's sculpture, our late loved ones would present a lightness of spirit. There is a similar tradition in Christian culture: Saint Michael, the archangel who cast Satan out of Hell, was also responsible for the weighing of souls, the measuring of sin in those who sought a place in Heaven.

This English pre-Reformation stained-glass panel depicts a moment from the Last Judgment (fig. 63). Common to all Abrahamic religions, the Last Judgment is believed to be a moment that will coincide with the Second Coming of Christ, when judgment is passed on all of humanity. In early fifteenth-century Europe, these kinds of vivid, terrifying scenes of cosmic reckoning would have been common in churches. Here, a man prays, begs for mercy as his sins are weighed and measured against Satan himself. And although he pleads, it is already too late: the sins have been committed, counted, and this is the moment of ultimate reckoning. The scales do not lie. It is a ruthlessly vivid image, designed to shock a congregation, to scare, to terrify us into goodness.

A century after the creation of the stained-glass panel, Albrecht Dürer, the German Renaissance artist, began work on a series of moralizing prints. *The Knight, Death and the Devil* (1513) is one of Dürer's *Meisterstiche*, or 'master prints' (fig. 64). It is perhaps the finest of three truly astonishing engravings that were intended not only to define a new standard of European print-making, but also to emphatically set out a moral framework. Created for popular consumption, *The Knight, Death and the Devil* is quite literal: a knight, mature in years, rides through a rocky valley. In the far distance is a hilltop castle, perhaps the knight's destination, maybe a symbolic Jerusalem, but probably the place he has just departed. Although he is travelling with his loyal, faithful dog and on a magnificent horse, although he is suited in armour with a sword on his hip and a lance in his hand, he seems downcast and vulnerable. He is hunted, haunted: the Devil is at his heels, and Death is at his shoulder. Death carries an hourglass, and the sand is running out. From the look on the old knight's face, he knows it too. He is hounded by life, harassed by memories. He doesn't need the Devil to remind him of what is inevitable; and yet, against the challenges, the obstacles, he soldiers on. Dürer's print is about moral courage, stoicism, stamina and the inner strength required to find one's own path, to resist the temptation to deviate, knowing the inevitable future. It draws on Psalm 23, the psalm of David, on the idea of keeping faith even in the bleakest of contexts; it is a stark but well-known narrative. In some ways, the knight is the antithesis of Thomas J. Price's figure in *A Place Beyond*.

In almost every culture, there have been variations on the figure of the knight: the weary traveller who encounters and is tempted by the Devil. In medieval Europe, there

64.
ALBRECHT DÜRER (1471–1528)
The Knight, Death and the Devil, 1513.
Engraving, ink on paper, 24.2 × 18.1 cm

65.
WILLIAM HOGARTH (1697–1764)
AND SIMON FRANCIS RAVENET (1706–1774)
The Toilette, from the series *Marriage-à-la-Mode*, c. 1745.
Engraving, print on paper

was a tradition of burying criminals, and those who had taken their own lives, beyond the boundary of the town or at a crossroads – a practice that would only have heightened the sense that home was safe and there were dangers abroad. But these intermediate, liminal places between home and the wider world came to be seen as symbolically complex. They were often regarded as conduits, as places beyond spiritual jurisdiction; places of evil, moral ambiguity, magic and sometimes even possibility.

In the 1900s, when jazz was searching for its own origin story, it would look to an encounter on a lonely road similar to that of Dürer's knight. But Robert Johnson, king of the blues, would broker an unnatural musical ability with the Devil in exchange for his soul. Part of art has always transgressed, has been risqué and dangerous. Later in the twentieth century, many musicians would follow Johnson: whole genres, albums, scores and bands would be dedicated to the occult and the Devil. It was a powerful mechanism designed to invert convention, to upturn belief systems and suggest the possibility of answers in the subversive. But within that inversion many musicians were ultimately seeking a moral coherence, their music often deployed as a means of mocking the piety, corruption and hypocrisies of the establishment.

William Hogarth grew up around London's Smithfield Market, one of the most deprived and demographically complex areas of the age. Smithfield was a potent microcosm of an ambitious, changing nation. Hogarth wanted to tell the stories of the streets, capture their hard lessons, record their endless victims and multiple hypocrisies, to hold up a mirror to the powerful and encourage popular debate. And he would turn his narrative canvases into accessible prints that could become contagious triggers for gossip, dissent and catharsis. *The Toilette* is part of Hogarth's six-painting series *Marriage-à-la-Mode*, which depicts an ill-conceived strategic marriage that destroys the lives of its protagonists and their families while revealing something of the culture of deceit, hypocrisy and greed of upper-middle-class and aristocratic society (fig. 65).

Moral creative statements such as this one would be a popular subject of the arts in a changing and unstable Europe for the next century, as figures from Charles Dickens to Gustave Flaubert, from Hogarth to George Cruikshank, captured and catalysed shifts in politics, social attitudes and purpose, pushing back against authority and conventional thinking to discover new ways of being. And when Flaubert's Madame Bovary said, '*Il ne faut pas toucher aux idoles: la dorure en reste aux mains*' (or, as it has been adopted in modern English parlance, 'Never meet your heroes, they are sure to disappoint you'), she spoke to and for the age. It was a comment on a time of dissolution, dissent, tumult and revolt – but also a time of empowerment, a time to seek purpose within.

The question of a museum's purpose and that of its collection is at the heart of V&A East. The permanent galleries explore why making matters, why things matter,

66.

HANY 'ABD AL-KADER

Second Revolution Khayamiya, 2011–12.
Textile panel, 250 × 250 cm

and how a collection of objects from across the creative disciplines can speak to the world today. We move from models of sustainable design rooted in the traditional knowledge of the Himalayan Institute of Alternatives in Ladakh to Cairo tent-maker Hany 'Abd al-Kader's subversive adaptation of decorative textiles into a record of civil uprising (fig. 66); from the trail-blazing designs of Vivienne Westwood to Takuya Sawada's reworking of national identity through Japanese fashion brand Takuya Angel, or the reflection of contemporary Britain in the costumes and designs of Keith Khan; to the rebuilding of Granby, a derelict neighbourhood in Liverpool that was revitalized by community-led action in collaboration with the London-based creative organization Assemble

67.

GRANBY WORKSHOP

Table lamp, 2015–16. Moulded Granby rock, 20.5 × 11.6 × 14 cm (fig. 67). Mixing global stories with those from East London, maker's voices are at the heart of an exploration into their individual and collective motivations. As in this book, a trans-historical approach brings together objects from diverse geographies, disciplines and time periods in the hope of weaving new narratives through serendipitous connections. Here we encounter the power of creativity to make people and systems visible; the breaking of boundaries, imagination and critical thinking; the observers who make sense of our world; making as a tool for resistance, solidarity and social change; design that is future-facing, meeting the challenges of our age, inspired by vernacular and indigenous traditions; creative agency and empowerment; and things that speak to our needs.

And, to return to where we started, perhaps that sense of purpose, of creative moral purpose, is what the young subject of *A Place Beyond* represents. Thomas J. Price cast in bronze a figure who looks with deliberation out towards the horizon but is ultimately introspective. While confident, she is focused inwardly on her own future. In the end, like so much great art, *A Place Beyond* is about possibility and potential, imagination and hope; about seeking external inspiration while excavating within to discover purpose; about allowing our creative imagination to prise open new apertures, helping us not only to cast new light on the world as we see it, but also to dream of worlds that we might yet make.

MAUD SULTER (1960–2008)

Urania (Portrait of Lubaina Himid), 1989

Dye-destruction print, 153 × 122 cm

This portrait of the artist Lubaina Himid is one of nine photographs that make up Maud Sulter's seminal photographic series *Zabat*. The series comprises prose poems alongside large-scale portraits of Sulter's creative contemporaries, collaborators and colleagues, each staged as a Greek muse, the scenes imbued with layers of symbolism relating to sisterhood, memory and history. Himid, who was Sulter's partner at one time, appears in *Zabat* as Urania, the muse of astrology. *Zabat* celebrates collaborative relationships and the creativity of Black women, whom the artist recognizes as systematically under-represented and under-acknowledged in the institutions of art and culture.

Epilogue

In the summer of 2025, I was offered the chance to meet one of my heroes, one of my childhood idols, and – in flagrant disregard of Madame Bovary – I took it. Joan Armatrading, the brilliant singer-songwriter, came to visit the V&A with her childhood guitar, which she was offering as a gift to the nation. As someone who had grown up on her music, had celebrated her hits and Grammy nominations, the chance to meet her was a career highlight. And as well as leaving the V&A her guitar, she left me with a story, a story of purpose.

'As a young child,' she began, 'my mother would walk me to school each morning and home each afternoon. Every trip, we would pass the same pawnbroker, its window full of orphaned objects left by people who had run out of choices.' One day, a guitar appeared in the window. Not a new and gleaming instrument, but an old, scratched, slightly sad guitar, which had been played close to destruction. It was the moment when Joan understood her purpose. She simply had to have it. She asked her mother if they could buy the guitar, knowing the answer: they could not afford the £3 price tag. But Joan desperately wanted the guitar and would ask her mother for it again and again, every time they passed the shop, until longing turned to need. Eventually, her mother's resistance broke, and they exchanged two unwanted prams for that old, rickety, lovely guitar.

Joan had found her tool of existential expression, and she would teach herself to play. It was more than a musical instrument, however; it would become an instrument

GUITAR OWNED BY
JOAN ARMATRADING (b. 1950)
Wood, 93.2 × 34 × 8.6 cm

of self-discovery, leading to a stellar career of performances and recordings, of awards and accolades, of hits and glorious reviews. But that pure, fundamental drive to create, make, perform, to share, would endure – her need for music as necessary as breath.

And that has been the core narrative of the preceding chapters: we humans simply need to create, and to spend time with creative excellence. And while we might construct museums and galleries as platforms for this purpose, a basic need to spend time with art is simply part of who and what we are. Creating and being among creativity are ancient drives. These were conventions that were created to bring about conversations about community and choice over millennia, to carry messages in ways that could overcome barriers of language and literacy; and although the creative traditions evolved, the essential need did not. As with so many of the varied practices that we have considered in this book, art and beautiful things are so often created and deployed to help us in the timeless task of communally making our case and communally making choices.

Perhaps that is what makes art so important: as conscious, sentient, empathetic beings, we humans don't just experience the world, we feel it. And, from birth, we develop a preternatural urge to share, to communicate, to set out our record, to leave something behind. What the arts have done uniquely well is in capturing not just a material record of the world around us, but a sense of how we and others feel. Time, language, difference and distance disappear in the face of the power of great art. Creativity can open up a shared space of communal consciousness that not only helps us make sense of the world, but inspires the kind of empathy that, at its most potent, aids healthy resolution and catharsis. It is understandable how this powerful compulsion, which is common to all of humanity, would become the critical medium for telling our story. As I hope this book has shown, art simply has an impact on every aspect of our lives – from the choices we make about our appearance, to the most affecting ways in which we express and explore our feelings about our health, property and security. Art has been fundamental to helping us build and inspire confidence and respect, maintain friendships and families, and feel safe and secure. But perhaps most potently, art, craft, design has informed the tenor of how we might live well together, the ethics and morality of the world as it is, and as we might wish it to be.

It is curious that we spend so much time trying to quantify the value of the arts – that we are so often asked to defend culture from accusations of being frivolous or a luxury. And yet, so many of the things we need in order to live well are framed and touched by the arts, by creativity. Art, culture and creativity have been our constant guide, our witness, our inspiration. Art has been a way-marker, reminding us of how high we might aim; a mirror that has captured our flaws, directed a light into the darkest corners of our histories to remind us of how, within our human story of weakness and vanity, there is also one of love and indefatigability and hope. When we have sought or questioned purpose, it is art that has so often provided us with the clearest mirror, the deepest level of analysis. The objects the archaeologists pull from ancient graves, the things we would choose to accompany us into infinity, are the beautiful, the useful, the loved.

NOTES

1 Empire Day, celebrated each year on 24 May, was created to inspire unity and patriotism across the British Empire.

2 This was a period when the Crown sold monopolies on the importation of exotic goods to wealthy courtiers, creating a deeply speculative and competitive environment in the royal court. There were, however, huge risks involved – spoliation, wars and piracy, high import taxes – and success was not guaranteed.

3 The Jacobite Risings were a series of attempts by the Scottish to regain their throne from the British.

4 Samuel Pepys, *The Diary of Samuel Pepys*, Wednesday 20 September 1665, https://www.pepysdiary.com/diary/1665/09/20/ (accessed March 2026).

5 Courtney Worrell *et al.*, 'The Physiological Impact of Viewing Original Artworks vs. Reprints: A Comparative Study', working paper/pre-print, 2025. For more information and to download a copy of the study, see https://www.artfund.org/our-purpose/news/first-of-its-kind-study-proves-positive-impact-of-art-on-the-body (accessed March 2026).

6 Helen Chatterjee and Guy Noble, *Museums, Health and Well-Being* (London: Routledge, 2013).

7 WHO Covid-19 Dashboard, *World Health Organization*, https://data.who.int/dashboards/covid19 (accessed March 2026).

8 Alexandra Bradbury *et al.*, 'The Role of the Arts during the COVID-19 Pandemic', 31 August 2021, https://www.artscouncil.org.uk/sites/default/files/download-file/UCL_Role_of_the_Arts_during_COVID_13012022_0.pdf (accessed November 2025).

9 *Ibid.*

10 Ed Decker, 'Can you Mend a Broken Heart Through the Arts?', *International Arts + Mind Lab*, https://www.artsandmindlab.org/heart-health-and-the-arts/ (accessed November 2025).

11 Lara Hailey, quoted in *Sewn Antidote* object record, Victoria and Albert Museum, https://collections.vam.ac.uk/item/O1611598/sewn-antidote-quilt-hailey-lara (accessed January 2026).

12 Personal communication with Mariam Rosser-Owen, Curator, Middle East, Asia Department, Victoria and Albert Museum, March 2021.

13 Damien Gayle, 'Disposable Face Masks Used During Covid Have Left Chemical Timebomb, Research Suggests', *The Guardian*, 8 September 2025, https://www.theguardian.com/environment/2025/sep/08/disposable-face-masks-covid-chemical-timebomb (accessed March 2026).

14 Samuel Pepys, *The Diary of Samuel Pepys*, Thursday 14 September 1665, https://www.pepysdiary.com/diary/1665/09/14/ (accessed March 2026).

15 Sergei Diaghilev, quoted in Jennifer Homans, *Apollo's Angels: A History of Ballet* (New York: Random House, 2010), p. 301.

16 Eric Walter White, *Stravinsky: The Composer and His Works*, 2nd edn (Berkeley: University of California Press, 1979), p. 35.

17 Marianne Williams Tobias, programme notes, Igor Stravinsky, *The Firebird*, Indianapolis Symphony Orchestra, 2017, https://www.indianapolissymphony.org/backstage/program-notes/stravinsky-the-firebird/ (accessed November 2025).

18 'Introducing Natalia Goncharova', Tate, https://www.tate.org.uk/art/artists/natalia-goncharova-1186/introducing-natalia-goncharova (accessed March 2026).

19 Stefanie Waldek, 'Meet Trailblazing Austrian Designer Margarete Schütte-Lihotzky, the Inventor of the Modern Kitchen', *Architectural Digest*, https://www.architecturaldigest.com/sponsored/story/meet-margarete-schutte-lihotzky

20 Margarete Schütte-Lihotzky, *Warum ich Architektin wurde* [Why I Became an Architect] (Vienna/Salzburg: Residenz Verlag: 2019), quoted in Waldek, 'Meet Trailblazing Austrian Designer Margarete Schütte-Lihotzky'.

21 Margarete Schütte-Lihotzky, quoted in Gwendolen Webster, 'Revisit: Frankfurt

Kitchen by Margarete Schütte-Lihotzky', *Architectural Review*, 10 January 2022, https://www.architectural-review.com/essays/revisit/revisit-frankfurt-kitchen (accessed March 2026).

22 Do Ho Suh, quoted in Rachel Spence, 'Do Ho Suh in Venice: The Lives of Others', *Financial Times*, 11 May 2018, https://www.ft.com/content/e7cc1056-51e5-11e8-84f4-43d65af59d43 (accessed March 2026).

23 Thomas Bowditch, *The Mission from Cape Coast Castle to Ashantee* (London, 1819).

24 Georg Wilhelm Friedrich Hegel, quoted in Robert Maynard Hutchins, ed., *Great Books of the Western World*, vol. 46, *Hegel* (Chicago: Encyclopaedia Britannica Inc., 1952), p. 196.

25 Garnet Joseph Wolseley, 1st Viscount Wolseley, quoted in Christopher Hibbert, *The Great Mutiny: India, 1857* (New York: Viking Press, 1978), p. 254.

26 Shahed Saleem, quoted in Christopher Turner, 'The Ramadan Pavilion by Shahed Saleem', V&A Blog, 27 February 2023, https://www.vam.ac.uk/blog/museum-life/the-ramadan-pavilion-by-shahed-saleem?srsltid=AfmBOopdEQES64NOGC1jg5DIz_fAiaXO5RR9LhDNrP9vDydkCexoufi (accessed December 2025).

27 *Ibid.*

28 Shahed Saleem, quoted in 'British Mosques & Decolonising Islamic Architecture, Shahed Saleem', *Bayt Al Fann*, https://www.baytalfann.com/post/british-mosques-decolonising-islamic-arcitecture-shahed-saleem (accessed March 2026).

29 Shahed Saleem, quoted in Turner, 'The Ramadan Pavilion by Shahed Saleem'.

30 Imane Ayissi, quoted in 'Asseulenn Collection', Victoria and Albert Museum, 9 May 2021, https://collections.vam.ac.uk/item/O1616481/asseulenn-collection-ensemble-imane-ayissi/ (accessed March 2026).

31 Herman Melville, *Moby Dick; or, the Whale* (London: Penguin, 2009), Chapter 93, 'The Castaway', p. 452.

32 *Ibid.*, pp. 453–54.

33 Fred Hoffman, 'The Defining Years: Notes on Five Key Works', in Marc Mayer (ed.), *Basquiat* (London: Merrell Publishers in association with the Brooklyn Museum, New York, 2005), p. 129.

34 Kenny Zulu Whitmore, quoted in Carrie Reichardt, 'Interview: Black Panther Kenny "Zulu" Whitmore', 8 June 2020, *Idler*, https://www.idler.co.uk/article/interview-black-panther-kenny-zulu-whitmore/.

35 Elizabeth Fry, *Observations on the Visiting, Superintending, and Government, of Female Prisoners* (Norwich, 1827), p. 60.

36 Conversation between Fine Cell Work and an anonymous contributor to the HMP Wandsworth Quilt, 20 March 2010, quoted in 'HMP Wandsworth Quilt', Victoria and Albert Museum, 28 July 2010, https://collections.vam.ac.uk/item/O1165208/hmp-wandsworth-quilt-quilt-hmp-wandsworth/ (accessed March 2026).

ACKNOWLEDGMENTS

I would like to thank Rebecca Fortey and Tom Windross for driving the early thinking on this book, at the stage when it was just a set of possibilities. I am especially grateful to Tom, who then took up the baton as we shaped the conceptual approach. And I am particularly indebted to the brilliant, dedicated and patient Hannah Newell, who then worked with me at every subsequent stage of this book; who has been there through each draft and has invested hugely in the development of the chapter narratives and has been fastidious on the detail. I am hugely grateful.

And I would like to thank my initial readers, Philip Watson from Thames & Hudson and Brendan Cormier and Joanna Norman from the V&A, who generously reviewed early iterations of the chapters and offered advice and encouragement. I am also grateful to all the expert readers: Kira d'Alburquerque, Nick Barnard, Martin Barnes, Victoria Bradley, Zorian Clayton, Rachel Dedman, Emily Hannam, Fuchsia Hart, Jenny Gaschke, Rosalie Kim, Reino Liefkes, Jane Pritchard, Rosalind McKever, Mary Redfern, Jessica Rosenthal McGrath, Mariam Rosser-Owen, Marta Weiss, Masami Yamada, Christopher Wilk and colleagues from across the V&A, who read, advised and supported. You inspire me with your dedication and brilliance every single day.

At Thames & Hudson, thanks are also due to Mark Ralph, the book's project editor; to Karolina Prymaka and Matt Watson Young, its designers; to Jane Harman in production; and to Julie Hrischeva and Julian Honer for their ongoing support.

Lastly, I would like to thank and dedicate this book to art teachers: you have played such important roles in my life. I have a very vivid memory of crying into Miss Marshall's handkerchief when I learned the news that I had failed to gain an art scholarship at the age of twelve. She was my first art teacher, and she had been there through every important phase of my early creative development and was there for my first significant disappointment. And I am deeply grateful to Mr Griffiths, who taught me art at O level. He taught most effectively by being an enormously gifted artist himself, creating dazzling canvases in the classroom. He opened my 14-year-old eyes to what talent and dedication might look like. And lastly, I cannot forget Mr Cox, who tutored me at A level. Mr Cox was simply the cleverest human being I had ever met, and his uncompromisingly moral view of the world triggered something within me that I have tried to hold on to.

This wonderful group of teachers gave me the tools that would secure my entry into art school – and so begin a career. I am grateful to you all, and to all art teachers for inspiring creativity where it is needed most. As we saw earlier in the book, part of my role at V&A East has been to visit almost a hundred schools to talk about the value of the arts, to listen to young people talking about their own creative aspirations and, of course, to meet their teachers. This valuable time in schools only helped to reinforce my respect for all teachers of art, many working in environments where the subject is not a curriculum priority, but working nevertheless to inspire the young. Thank you.

PICTURE CREDITS

l = left; r = right; t = top; b = bottom; c = centre
Unless otherwise stated, images are © Victoria and Albert Museum, London.

9 V&A: T.427-1967. Given by Miss Caroline Combe. Courtesy Balenciaga; **17** V&A Archive: MA/22/A0046; **25l, r** V&A: IS.1943&A-1883; **25c** V&A: S.155-1886. Purchased from the Colonial and Indian Exhibition held in London in 1886; **32l** V&A: E.1861:98-1991; **32r** V&A: T.156-2016; **35** V&A: T.264-1966. Given by Mrs Olive Furnivall; **36** V&A: T.2457:1-2021. © Rahemur Rahman; **41t** V&A: T.178-1989. Given by the makers. © The McNish Trust; **41b** V&A T.444-1999. Given by Heal & Son Ltd. © The McNish Trust; **42** V&A: T.2429-2021. © ORANGE CULTURE NIGERIA; **49** V&A:1131-1864; **52** V&A: T.59-1935. Given by Col. F. G. G. Bailey; **54** V&A: T.106-2021. Given by the artist. © Lara Hailey; **57** V&A: T.81-2021. Gift of Jonathan Anderson. © Liv Huffman; **59** V&A: ME.16-2021. Presented by Art Fund. © Bita Ghezelayagh; **60** V&A: ME.22-2021. Presented by Art Fund. © Esam Ali; **63** V&A: CD.52-2021. Given by Cristian Fracassi – Isinnova SRL. Courtesy ISINNOVA; **64** V&A: M.805-1926. Lt. Col. G. B. Croft-Lyons Bequest; **68** Collection Wereldmuseum Rotterdam: WM-28566; **73** V&A: IS.54-2005. Given by M. E. Liggett; **74** V&A: E.257-2005. Purchased through the Julie and Robert Breckman Print Fund. © 2025 Susie (Balgo) Bootja Bootja/Copyright Agency. Licensed by DACS; **77** V&A: W.674:1 to 4-2001. Given by the designers. © Dunne & Raby; **78** V&A: PH.1157-1980; **80** V&A: E.637-2014. Purchase funded by the Photographs Acquisition Group; **82–83** V&A: A.30-1930. Given by Art Fund; **84** V&A: IM.159-1929. Given by Hon. Sir Arthur Lawley; **90** V&A: S.316-1978. Given by the Friends of the Museum of the Performing Arts © 2025 Succession Picasso/DACS, London; **93** V&A: S.562A-1983. © 2025 Succession Picasso/DACS, London; **96** V&A: E.287-1961. © Natalia Goncharova/UPRAVIS, 2026; **101** V&A: S.455-1980. © Natalia Goncharova/UPRAVIS, 2026; **102** V&A: T.81-2022. © Christian Ovonlen; **111** V&A: W.15:1 to 89-2005. Courtesy the Margarete Schütte-Lihotzky Centre; **115** V&A: CD.26-2018; **116** V&A: E.503-2022. © Do Ho Suh. Digital images courtesy the artist; **118–19** V&A: E.2748 to 2751-2016. © Jessie Brennan. Photograph courtesy the artist; **120** V&A: E.21-2006. Purchased through the Julie and Robert Breckman Print Fund. © 2025 Sonia Boyce. All Rights Reserved, DACS; **123** V&A: E.407-1998. Purchased through the Cecil Beaton Royalties Fund. © Tom Hunter; **127** V&A: M.1135-1926; **132** V&A: T.208-1969; **135t** V&A: CIRC.706-1969; **135b** V&A: 5-1875; **136t** The British Museum: Af1900,0427.1. Photograph © The Trustees of the British Museum; **136b** The Wallace Collection: OA1683. Photograph © Wallace Collection, London, UK/Bridgeman Images; **139t** V&A: 369-1874; **139b** V&A: 370-1874; **142** V&A: M.13-2020. Purchased through the generosity of William & Judith, Douglas and James Bollinger. © Emefa Cole; **145** V&A: E.163:7-2009. Purchased through the generous support of the Friends of the V&A. © 2025 Hew Locke. All rights reserved, DACS; **151** V&A: W.54-1928. Given by Viscount Lascelles; **154** V&A: 407-1905; **159t** V&A: E.1046-2019. Given by the artist. © Shahed Saleem; **162** V&A: T.2435:1,2-2021. Purchase funded by the American Friends of the V&A through the generosity of Diana Quasha. © Imane Ayissi/Cinq Six Sept; **163** V&A: T.2436:1 to 3-2021. Given by Imane Ayissi. © Imane Ayissi/Cinq Six Sept; **165** V&A: T.275-2019. © Given by Gucci 2020; **166** V&A: T.258-2019. Courtesy Off-White by Virgil Abloh; **173** Museum of Fine Arts, Boston: 99.22. Photograph © 2026 Museum of Fine Arts, Boston; **176** V&A: CD.8-2023. Given by the artist. © Greg Bunbury; **179** V&A: E.2753-2016. Given by the artist. © Esther Rolinson; **180** V&A: C.20-1995. Purchased with Alastair Pilkington Funds. © Emma Woffenden; **183** V&A: CD.59-2021. Courtesy Zhijun Wang and Yutong Duan; **184** V&A: CIRC.18-1972. Given by Avondale Mills Inc.; **189** © 2025 Ibrahim El-Salahi, courtesy Vigo Gallery. All rights reserved, DACS. Digital image, The Museum of Modern Art, New York/Scala, Florence; **192** V&A: M.3:1 to 3-2018. Courtesy Kenny 'Zulu' Whitmore; **195** National Gallery of Australia, Canberra: irn: 119802. Gift of Les Hollings and the Australian Textiles Fund 1989. Photograph © National Gallery of Australia, Kamberri/Canberra; **196** V&A: T.27-2010. © Fine Cell Work; **199** V&A: E.59-2021. Purchased with support from Art Fund and a legacy donation from Dr Philip da Costa. © Kehinde Wiley; **202** V&A: ME.15-2022. Given by the artist. © Sofia Karim; **206** V&A: T.43-2008. Supported by the Friends of the V&A. © Natasha Kerr; **209t** V&A: T.6-2008. Collection given by Edward Nugée QC; **209c** V&A: T.7, 8-2008. Collection given by Edward Nugée QC; **209b** V&A: T.4:1, 2-2008. Collection given by Edward Nugée QC;

210 V&A: T.229-1999. Given by Mrs Alison Coate; **212** V&A: C.30:1 to 9-2020. © Mawuena Kattah; **213** V&A: CIRC.321-1964. Bequeathed by Miss Mary Kirby; **214** V&A: E.236-2013. Purchased with the support of the National Lottery Heritage Fund and the Photographs Acquisition Group. © 2025 Yinka Shonibare CBE. All Rights Reserved, DACS; **217** V&A: B.78:1-1995. Gift of M. Harty; **218** V&A: E.362-2011. Supported by the National Lottery Heritage Fund. © Gavin Watson; **221** V&A: IS.29-2015. Given by Jasjit Kaur Sidhu in memory of her grandmother Basant Kaur Sandhu (née Jeuni Kaur Sidhu); **222** V&A: T.124-1988. Given by Jessica Teresa Cloudesley-Savorelli; **227** The Museum of Modern Art, New York: Purchase. Acc. n.: 130.1946.a-c. © 2025 DACS. Digital image, The Museum of Modern Art, New York/ Scala, Florence; **228** © 2025 Salvador Dalí, Fundació Gala-Salvador Dalí, DACS. Photograph courtesy Sotheby's; **233** British Museum: Am.8231.Photograph © The Trustees of the British Museum; **234** V&A: 1288-1874; **237** V&A: IM.173-1910. Purchased from the dealer Mr Imre Schwaiger; **238–39** V&A: C.2258&A-1910. Bequeathed by George Salting, Esq.; **241** V&A: C.2257-1910. Bequeathed by George Salting, Esq.; **244** © Thomas J. Price. Courtesy the artist and Hauser & Wirth. Photograph: Keith Lubow; **246** V&A: C.164-1929; **249** V&A: E.595-1940. Bequeathed by Miss Alice G. E. Carthew; **250** V&A: DYCE.2753. Bequeathed by Rev. Alexander Dyce; **253** V&A: ME.4-2016. Presented by Art Fund. © Hany Al-Sayed Ahmad Abd Al-khader; **254** V&A: CD.143-2016. Courtesy Granby Workshop; **257** V&A: E.1793-1991. © 2025 Estate of Maud Sulter. All rights reserved, DACS; **260** V&A: S.525-2025. Given by Joan Armatrading

INDEX

Illustrations are in *italics*.

For my dear late brother Joe – in deepest gratitude for all you did and continue to do to inspire me

First published in the United Kingdom in 2026 by Thames & Hudson Ltd, 6–24 Britannia Street, London WC1X 9JD, in association with the Victoria and Albert Museum, London

First published in the United States of America in 2026 by Thames & Hudson Inc., 500 Fifth Avenue, New York, New York 10110

EU Authorized Representative: Interart S.A.R.L.
19 rue Charles Auray, 93500 Pantin, Paris, France
productsafety@thameshudson.co.uk
interart.fr

A CIP catalogue record for this book is available from the British Library

Library of Congress Control Number 2026938246

ISBN 978-0-500-48122-6
01

Printed in China by RR Donnelley

FSC
www.fsc.org
MIX
Paper | Supporting responsible forestry
FSC® C144853